TRANSFORMING YOUR COMMUNITY
Empowering for Change

The Professional Practices in Adult Education and Human Resource Development Series explores issues and concerns of practitioners who work in the broad range of settings in adult and continuing education and human resource development.

The books are intended to provide information and strategies on how to make practice more effective for professionals and those they serve. They are written from a practical viewpoint and provide a forum for instructors, administrators, policy makers, counselors, trainers, managers, program and organizational developers, instructional designers, and other related professionals.

Editorial correspondence should be sent to the Editor-in-Chief:

Michael W. Galbraith
Florida Atlantic University
Department of Educational Leadership
College of Education
Boca Raton, FL 33431

TRANSFORMING YOUR COMMUNITY

Empowering for Change

Allen B. Moore
and
Rusty Brooks

KRIEGER PUBLISHING COMPANY
MALABAR, FLORIDA
1996

Original Edition   1996

Printed and Published by
KRIEGER PUBLISHING COMPANY
KRIEGER DRIVE
MALABAR, FLORIDA 32950

Library of Congress Cataloging-in-Publication Data

Moore, Allen B.
    Transforming your community : empowering for change / Allen B.
Moore and Rusty Brooks. — Original ed.
        p.   cm. — (The professional practices in adult education and
human resource development series)
    Includes bibliographical references and index.
    ISBN 0-89464-899-3 (alk. paper)
    1. Rural development—Georgia.   2. Rural development—United
States.   3. Community development—Georgia.   4. Community
development—United States.   5. Regional planning—Georgia.
6. Regional planning—United States.   I. Brooks, Rusty.   II. Title.
III. Series.
HN79.G43C66   1996
307'.1'412'09758—dc20   96-14555
                                                            CIP

10   9   8   7   6   5   4   3   2

CONTENTS

PREFACE

As we travel, visit with community groups, and talk with colleagues at professional meetings, we have become increasingly aware that our view of community economic development is distinctly different from others. An important reason we put this book together is because we believe in and practice a "bottom-up action learning/action planning" approach to community economic development. Some of our professional colleagues have become impatient with community involvement strategies and want to dictate, or use, a "top-down" or "expert" strategy because they see it as more expedient and more "informed" than the slower bottom up idea.

Another reason for putting this book together was to organize some of our collective ideas and merge them with what we think has been working in communities and to seek reactions from peers, colleagues, and critics regarding this community economic development approach. We do not believe there is only "one way" to develop a community and that is our strategy in this book. What we are saying is that there are many different ideas, projects, strategies, and actions that have produced what residents were looking for . . . whether it was change, development, community improvements, or general improvements to quality of life.

Community economic development is a catchall phrase. It includes almost anything that an individual, a group, or a collection of leaders say they want to accomplish in the name of improvements, change, enhanced quality of life, and jobs. One of our Institute of Community and Area Development (ICAD) colleagues calls it " . . . putting a little jingle (money) in their pockets." We have explained why we see community development and economic development as a unified concept. We believe strongly in people doing for themselves what others cannot or will not do. To be successful at "doing for themselves," individuals and groups must learn about what they want to do, how to achieve their goals, and how to put their collective wisdom together for a specific purpose or outcome.

ACKNOWLEDGMENTS

We wish to thank community groups in Georgia, neighboring states, and throughout the United States, Mexico, and Canada for providing us the opportunity to visit, discuss, and follow up on community economic development strategies and results. We have, individually and collectively, worked with over 500 communities in the past 20 years developing and promoting community economic development activities.

We want to especially thank Joe Whorton, Director of the Institute of Community and Area Development (ICAD), and S. E. Younts, Vice President for Services at the University of Georgia, for providing the opportunities for us to work with a variety of community groups and organizations. Two people assisted us by reading drafts of this book and offering numerous suggestions for improvement. We extend special appreciation to Pat Merritt of Oglethorpe Power Corporation in Atlanta, Georgia, and Paul Hardy of the Institute of Community and Area Development at the University of Georgia. George Dick endured countless hours of our bantering about editors' comments and other issues related to the book.

We also want to acknowledge assistance in word processing and graphic design by Michelle Eberhart, Kim Saxon, and Sandy Phillips. Our special thanks to them.

Finally, we dedicate this book to those who have helped us learn about community economic development: community residents, colleagues, associates, clients, and families who live in small towns and rural areas where they had to do their own development out of necessity.

We want to single out some special people who had to take care of many and varied everyday demands while we were visiting communities. This is for Anne, Paula, Ty, and Kelsey. Thanks for your support!

THE AUTHORS

Allen B. Moore is associate professor of adult education joint staffed with the Department of Adult Education and the Institute of Community and Area Development at the University of Georgia in Athens. He received his B.S. degree (1964) in forest management, a master's degree (1968) in forestry, and his Ed.D. (1970) in adult education from North Carolina State University at Raleigh.

Moore's main research and writing activities have focused on human capital development related to participation in continuing education, staff development, and community adult education. He has written numerous journal articles, book chapters, and monographs, and has presented papers on career development, rural adult education, and community economic development. He is an active member of the Georgia Adult Education Association (GAEA), from which he received in 1989 the distinguished service award and in 1994, along with coauthor James Feldt, received the literary award for their book *Facilitating Community and Decision-Making Groups*. He is also a member of the International Community Development Society. Since 1986 he has conducted numerous instructional programs and long-range planning retreats for nonprofit community boards and groups. He and Rusty Brooks, since 1991, have conducted intensive instructional and resource referral sessions for community groups as part of the Community Economic Development Program (CEDP) at the University of Georgia.

Rusty Brooks is an associate professor at the University of Georgia. His appointment is in the Institute of Community and Area Development where he works primarily on community economic development, action planning, and decision conferencing for public and private sector organizations. He earned a B.A. and M.C.J. from the University of Alabama and his Ph.D. in sociology from the University of Georgia.

He has authored over 100 community-level studies in Georgia and has worked with recent clients such as the Georgia Power Company, numerous chambers of commerce, the Council of Economic Development Organizations, the Atlanta Regional Commission, the Southeastern Regional Directors Institute, and the Georgia Department of Transportation, among others, in developing strategic plans. He served on the Rural Advisory Committee for the Southern Growth Policies Board study, *After the Factories.* He also served on the 1983 United States Department of Agriculture task force which developed *Rural Development: A Commitment to Change.* He recently served on the Southern Rural Development Center Committee on Infrastructure Investment which in 1990 produced the monograph, *Innovative Infrastructure Financing and Delivery Systems.* He has also published his work in *Southern Rural Sociology, Journal of the Community Development Society, Broiler Industry Review, Extension Review, the Rural Sociologist, the Southern Journal of Agricultural Economics,* and *the Journal of Agribusiness.* He is a past president of the Southern Rural Sociological Association, a former book review editor for the Journal of the Community Development Society, and has served on major committees for the Rural Sociological Society.

INTRODUCTION

In 1991 and 1992 the authors were given the task of putting together a learning experience for adults to promote community economic development. The results of this effort became the Community Economic Development Program (CEDP), a unique educational approach to facilitating community team-based efforts in designing local economic development initiatives. We were not given a set of limitations or constraints but were encouraged to conduct a nationwide search of innovative community economic development programs, talk to people, observe programs, participate in meetings, and involve colleagues from universities and the private sector in designing the experience(s).

We saw this as an opportunity to put together something for community groups not currently being served (i.e., community volunteers who do much of the work for local agencies and organizations). It was also an opportunity to put together activities with followup strategies. We were informed through our visits, interviews, and observations that follow-up was the most neglected aspect of many educational events and change programs for communities.

We selected small communities in rural regions of Georgia that had been left behind by statewide community economic developers. We found that, in the view of some statewide economic developers, the perception was that "nothing was going on in those communities so why bother working with them." Well we visited, observed, listened, and discussed what they were doing and what they would like to do to improve their area. We found out that a great many things, activities, and projects were underway in these communities. What these groups lacked was someone to encourage them, offer them information and ideas, share experiences from other communities, and help them organize their participants (i.e., their energy sources) into workforce units that added up to a unified goal.

During 1994, the governor's office in Georgia promoted a regional approach to economic development and used the model, processes, and strategies from the Community Economic Development Program (CEDP) as an implementation guide. Fostering regional actions and projects, which must overcome political boundaries, turf, local politics, and a host of other issues, is possible if residents and elected officials want change. In some states, including Georgia, legislation has been adopted to enable communities, counties, and elected bodies to band together in collaborative ventures for community economic development.

YOUR "IDEA WAGON"

As one participant at the CEDP said, "You have loaded our idea wagon and now it is up to us to take this information and put it to use in our community." We have tried to load your idea wagon about the many possibilities and challenges that face groups as they move from talking to taking action in their communities. We have also tried to organize the information in a meaningful way. In each chapter we have provided personal examples with names of real people who implemented a particular activity or strategy. We have also written up case examples of our perceptions about what did or did not happen in a particular community. Specific ICAD or related reports have cited, in detail, the activities of community groups as they designed, implemented, and followed up on a project. Also, we believe that each chapter makes a contribution to the overall learning process so we have included "tips for getting started" to facilitate the reader thinking about how this or that activity might be implemented in their town.

APPLYING OUR PERSPECTIVE
TO COMMUNITIES

The transformation framework (Chapter 1) explains how community groups and leaders can develop and promote ideas and actions for community economic development. In addition, it describes how community leaders and groups can put the framework we outline to use in their towns. We propose several approaches to using the framework for enhancing local community economic development.

It has been our experience that most of the activities discussed in this book are interrelated and in some cases dependent upon each other. However for the purposes of analysis and discussion, we have separated out various concepts, like community economic development, to emphasize their importance and propose ways to put these ideas into action (Chapter 2). Chapter 3, Education, Training, and Organizing Community Volunteers, emphasizes how communities can get started in their community economic development efforts. For example, we illustrate how community groups, interested leaders, and concerned citizens inform, organize, educate, and train themselves to get the job done. Government regulations and quality of life and environmental concerns (Chapter 4) are high on resident priority lists when anyone proposes change and development. Transforming communities is a process of becoming aware of these regulations, addressing challenges, looking for options, and involving residents in maintaining and improving their quality of life.

We see another aspect of development that can involve changing and revitalizing your community's downtown (Chapter 5), attracting out-of-town visitors to historic, recreation, and unique sites in the community (Chapter 6). Again, this book discusses what this type of activity implies for maintaining or improving resident quality of life.

Other approaches to community economic development have emphasized "maintaining what we have." We encourage communities to pay significant attention to supporting and expanding business retention efforts and job creation strategies in their community (chapter 7). How communities fund and support their discussions, analysis, planning, implementation, and follow up on specific community economic development projects is a critical element of our framework for action learning/action planning (Chapter 8). Communities may operate with local contributions, gifts from benefactors, or they can organize and systematically beg, borrow, and search out funding sources sympathetic to their needs. Some communities have applied nontraditional or special marketing approaches to community economic development when telecommunications, arts, festivals, historical, and cultural venues offer other ways of promoting community economic development (Chapter 9).

For almost all communities, there is a need to increase resource capacity and build networks with agencies, individuals, and associations to multiply the potential of an area (Chapter 10). Sometimes this is done in regional groups of cities, towns, and counties. In other situations it has resulted in telecommunications networks both locally and internationally.

We believe that all of these applications of our framework for community economic development must have a "future orientation" (Chapter 11). We strongly suggest that communities capitalize on their existing resources that can be improved or repositioned in some way to anticipate some future demand or trend. It is more than star gazing and dreaming. It is putting the collective vision of individuals to work for the community and region.

What we envision for this book is a working framework with real examples of communities working on their vision for change. In the past 20 years we have worked with over 500 communities, counties, and jurisdictions to put their energy, expertise, vision, and action learning projects to the test. We provide case examples of how some of these have worked and how they have failed in transforming communities. We are looking forward to the journey and we want you to travel with us as we explore communities, cities, towns, rural crossroads, and neighborhoods.

CHAPTER 1

Framework for Community Economic Development

In the past several decades, especially since 1950, researchers and practitioners have proposed a myriad of approaches and techniques for involving individuals, groups, agencies, and governments in community action, economic development, and community improvements. Autocratic, "top-down" directives have given way to empowering individuals and using a "bottom-up" approach. For example, Paulo Freire (1968) has designed, implemented, and promoted an empowering process of dialogue and learning for adults. Through his dialogue approach he has empowered individuals living in remote villages in Brazil. The dialogue approach encourages these natives to describe living and working conditions through the creation of drawings and other visual techniques that illustrate their everyday life—their relationships with the land, other landowners, nature, and their families. Through their drawings and other visuals the natives portray what is happening to these native people and why it is happening. What they discuss around their drawings and visuals becomes the content and lessons for learning how to read and write their language. They shift from using pictures of others to discussing their own living and working conditions as it emerges from the visuals. The discussions and dialogue become additional content for reading and writing exercises. New situations and pending changes in the country or district or village generate new dialogue and so learning, and learning about change, takes place. Freire's work provides one of the foundation blocks for our work with community groups.

LEARNING AND
TRANSFORMATION PROCESSES

We extensively utilize Mezirow's (1978) conceptual ideas in defining our framework. Mezirow considers learning and change to be the result of an individual being confronted by a new social role, frustration with changing social norms, or new meaning attached to old cultural symbols. These conditions and situations, become for Mezirow, the basis for an individual's *disorienting dilemma* in their life or community. More everyday examples of a disorienting dilemma might include learning to drive an automobile, becoming a parent and taking care of a newborn child, finding a job, or bringing more and new employment opportunities to the community. Mezirow's disorienting dilemma belongs to the individual and he suggests that the dilemma must be recognized, discussed and resolved, following Friere's (1968) dialogue. Resolving the dilemma is the action learning process engaged in by individuals and groups and which we describe in this book.

In a recent educational workshop that we managed, one of our economic development friends used an interesting metaphor to describe the disorienting dilemma idea. His metaphor revolved around the idea of what he called community "ugly babies." This speaker, a very well-respected fellow in economic development circles, is most adept at using what might best be called colloquial metaphors to describe economic development situations and problems. In this particular instance he used the very personal experience of viewing someone else's baby for the first time.

A baby is a very innocent creature which everyone finds difficulty in criticizing, especially in the presence of its parents. Parents are also reluctant to admit that their baby may be less than attractive, for parents tend to believe that their baby is the most beautiful baby in the world. Even parents who may reluctantly admit that their baby may not be the most beautiful baby will nevertheless go to great ends to make their baby attractive. We spend great amounts of money on clothes and ribbons to make our baby presentable and pleasing to the eye.

In many respects, our individual communities are our babies. We are sometimes reluctant to admit problems with how presentable our "baby," our community, is to others. His metaphor of the ugly baby points out that all communities have some elements, which can be organizational, visual, and/or personal, that mitigate against successful community development activities or that convey an impression to outsiders that the community is not a successful or prosperous community. He wanted communities to recognize that these elements are disorienting dilemmas, or as he called them ugly babies. The metaphor of ugly babies is used to emphasize that people are reluctant to say, "My goodness, that is an 'ugly baby'!" We know that not all babies, or parts of towns, or civic organizations, or people in leadership roles are beautiful or helpful, constructive, attractive, etc. Therefore, communities must recognize that they have a problem and that they do have a point of departure for change, improvement, or transformation. Sometimes we have to put more attractive clothes on our baby or put a bright ribbon in their hair. We believe the group or community or organization many times needs help in beginning the discussion or raising the subject about disorienting dilemmas and community ugly babies. Once a process is put in place to get this done, the dialogue and discussion can proceed and action learning can begin.

Most of our understanding and application of action learning comes from Revans (1980). Beginning with his work in 1945 with coal miners in England, he has written extensively about action learning. Action learning is based on the premise that there is no learning without action and no real action without learning by those implementing a change (Pedler, 1991). Action learning, according to Pedler, is based upon definition and redefinition of problems. Individuals concerned about problems, issues, or disorienting dilemmas work to define and resolve these situations. It is a basic assumption about human interactions that problems cannot exist unless someone knows, cares, and can do something about the problems or issues. Solving a given problem however is not an end in itself. What is achieved by the group is learning — they have learned to problem-solve—and this process can be applied to other issues or situations. As the group discusses, defines, redefines, seeks solutions, tries out options, and has setbacks and successes, they see themselves and the problem change.

Learning new information, confirming existing experiences, and deciding on a course of action are all transforming processes for adults. Mezirow (1978), Revans (1980), and others connect the transformation process with deliberate action—action to problem-solve or change. Another assumption in this action learning process is that people from all levels of the organization or community must be aware of, involved in, and supportive of the shared vision for change.

ASKING KEY QUESTIONS

Pedler (1991) cites Revans (1980) as continuously asking three key questions, the "Triad," of any group addressing any problem. Revans' Triad is related to helping define some particular problem.

Revans' Triad

1. Who knows about the problem?

2. Who cares about it?

3. Who can do something about it?

We extend the Revans' Triad to include additional questions that we believe help groups better frame the questions which can result in defining problems more clearly:

1. Who creates the problem?

2. Who owns or has the problem? (Revans: Who knows about the problem?)

3. Who sends/transmits the problem?

4. Who receives/accepts the problem?

5. Who should/is mandated to respond to the problem?

6. Who wants to solve the problem? (Revans: Who cares about it?)

7. Who decides about options/solutions to the problem? (Revans: Who can do something about it?)

8. Who implements problem solutions?

9. Who evaluates options/solutions implemented?

10. Who follows up with evaluations?

11. Who uses implementations/evaluations to generate new problems/issues?

Answers to these and other questions begin to identify participants in the action learning and problem solving processes. We draw other support for these questions from the work of James Yen, reported on by the extensive research of Lam (1993) who proposes "Credos" of James Yen.

Credos of Yen

1. Go to the people

2. Live among the people

3. Learn from the people

4. Plan with the people

5. Work with the people

6. Start with what the people know

7. Build on what the people have

8. Teach by showing; learn by doing

9. Not a showcase but a pattern

10. Not odds and ends but a system

11. Not piecemeal but an integrated approach

12. Not to conform but to transform

13. Not relief but release

From our action learning perspective these credos are critical guides to our work with community groups. To best illustrate our philosophy, both theoretically and conceptually, we have rewritten the James Yen Credos in the following way:

> Start with where people are (i.e., their dilemma, situation) and build upon what resources and knowledge they have by engaging them in discussion (i.e., action learning). Learning and teaching about dilemmas can be done by examining patterns, systems, and approaches and by continuously asking key questions of the group. The group changes or transforms both the problem and themselves by examining what they have learned in their journey.

EMPOWERING TO SOLVE PROBLEMS

We believe the Credos (Yen as reported by Lam, 1993) are important guides to empowering adults to solve their own problems and design their futures. Gaventa (1980) describes how residents in an Appalachian community came together and organized their efforts into a learning and social action group. They were concerned about sick and dying residents in the community. They learned how to organize themselves to gather and chemically analyze water samples from what they believed was a polluted stream. They used this knowledge to demand that solid waste dumping be halted and controlled to prevent hazardous chemical runoff into streams and ground water. This is an example of how groups organize and empower themselves for change regarding a dilemma that dramatically affected their community.

Sanders (1966), Warren (1978), Wilkinson (1991), and Nix (1977) have described ways of using a social planning action process in a community setting to bring about learning and change. Briefly, a social planning action process may be described as examining the past and current situation in a group or community to define a need or problem. An idea for change may be proposed or initiated by an individual or group. Existing community leaders, elected public officials and influential people support or legitimize the idea. Solutions for the idea or issue are proposed and communicated within the group or community. Public reactions and suggestions for improving the idea are sought. Specific actions to implement the idea are encouraged. Individuals and groups evaluate results, and new ideas or issues emerge.

What we are suggesting is to connect some of the social planning action processes with action learning processes to engage, empower, energize, and challenge community members to learn and remember how they successfully resolve problems — their disorienting dilemmas. The social planning action process is not greatly different from Stewart's (1991) seven S's (structure, strategy, systems, skills, shared values, staff, and style) and Carnall's (1990) universal "gap" model of change that involves the "journey of transition" from the current situation/condition to a new or desired state/condition. The journey of transition encourages learning, change, and social action.

LINKAGE TO COMMUNITY
AND ECONOMIC DEVELOPMENT

Sanders (1966) points out that community development grew out of a union of community organization, which stresses local action and local resources, and economic development, which includes planning and systematic movement toward defined goals. We also suggest that much, if not all, community and economic development efforts involve adult community members and have a direct relationship to adult education or action learning. We see direct benefits to community and economic development that results from learning (adult education and action learning); community organization (involving adults from throughout the community); dialogue and discussion (involvement and empowerment); action (action planning and action learning); and follow up (reviewing actions and seeking new dilemmas or goals).

Our approach to community and economic development is to involve people from all backgrounds and interests from the community to discuss and reflect on community and economic development actions. We do not believe the process should be expert driven but that it should be informed by expert knowledge and related information and the personal experiences of the group or community being affected. We bring groups together to share their vision of change and quality of life for the future. We see this future orientation as important to the success of action planning by groups. All too often we see groups who take on problems or tasks as becoming bogged down in what we call the *chronological planning trap* (Figure 1.1).

Many community groups brought together for some planning or problem solving purpose become past-oriented and spend a great deal of planning energy on events that have already happened and are out of their direct control (event A). Others get caught up in focusing on events or problems that are again outside their control in terms of framing the question, the debate, or the policy. Further, the circumstance or consequences around the event or problem are quickly approaching some sort of conclusion (event B). Still, other groups find themselves frantically trying to plan for some event or problem that is happening as they plan (event C). This is an occurrence that is all too frequent among planning groups. All three of these lead to frustrations and lack of planning success by groups. Our orientation is to move groups toward a future perspective (event D) through visioning exercises that link a futures orientation with action learning and action planning.

We find that Warren (1978) combines the two perspectives that we see as critical to successful community and economic development activity. Warren defined community development as the "deliberate attempt by community people to work to-

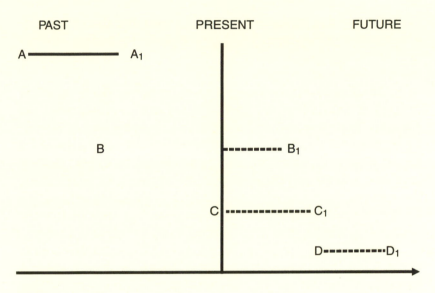

TIME

A, B, C, D = Decisions, Actions, Policies, Events

——————————— = Real Impacts and Results (What has happened?)

----------------- = Anticipated, Planned Impacts, and Results (What can happen?)

Figure 1.1 The chronological planning trap

gether to guide the future of their communities and the development of a corresponding set of techniques for assisting community people in such a process" (p. 20). This futures orientation (our visioning process) and the set of techniques we advocate (action learning and action planning) provide important parts of our framework for working with groups. From these group discussions emerge ideas and innovations that could have important impacts on the community. Local projects and interest in activities that can have regional (multi-community) impact bubble up from these discussions and reflections on what is needed to achieve the community's desired future.

PROCESS VERSUS CONTENT
PROCESS VERSUS PRODUCT

There are two additional issues that define the framework
for our work with community groups. The first involves the
question, or intellectual debate, of process versus content or
process versus product. We see this question, or debate, as a
bias against process, but, more importantly, as a bias against
process as an end in itself. Among academic and professional
community and economic development practitioners the debate
against process is shaped by a perception that process has no
research base or knowledge base. This debate defines process as
something practiced by those who are not fundamentally
schooled in the scientific method or professionally sound in
training or knowledge about the subject matter in which they
work. In many respects, we see bias against process as rooted in
a somewhat hypocritical perception by academics and professionals critical of process, that process approaches exclude experts because it empowers people to answer questions or solve
problems thereby posing a threat to *their* (the experts) exis-
tence. We argue that process should not be an end in itself but
a means to an end. Most importantly, we also see our process
approach as rooted in a research base and knowledge base that
comes from the action learning and adult education literature.

The other extension of this debate about process comes
from those who argue that process provides no product or outcome. Again, we argue that process, especially process that is
rooted in action learning and action planning, has products or
outcomes. Our belief is that successive products come from
groups that become adept at a process. Ross and Lappin (1967,
p. 15) defined process as an important end when they state that
" . . . the development of a specific project (such as an industry
or school) is less important than development of the capacity
of a people to establish that project." We encourage groups
to build on patterns of success that come out of their action
planning. An important component of our framework is that

groups have "early wins" that build momentum toward other accomplishments.

Along these lines, Sanders (1966, pp. 4–5) points out that community development can be viewed as a process, a method, a program, or a movement. Process is the important element here however. That element is further clarified by Cary (1970, p. 1) when he writes that " . . . beyond **emphasis** on process is alertness to the intangible effects on people, brought about through the process." "The **emphasis**," again referring to Sanders (1966, pp. 4–5), "is upon what happens to people psychologically and in their social relationships" as a result of a process. The process approach that we advocate is an orderly manner of proceeding to improve the community through the united efforts of the people in carrying out their own plans and programs.

We see other intangible benefits, or products and outcomes, from our "process work" with groups. We believe the process by which specific community organization or group decisions are put into action must be democratic, rational, and oriented toward the accomplishment of a specific task. The organization that undertakes this process carries a responsibility that goes unrecognized by many people. Bloomberg (1966, p. 374) points out that

> . . . there are no major formal organizations in the community which have as a central function the cultivation of citizenship. No institutional sector is devoted primarily to motivating participation in community affairs, developing the needed skills among the citizenry, and facilitating and organizing their involvement and participation in the recognition, definition, and resolution of community problems and issues.

Our idea of local democracy, of action learning in community groups, would therefore seem to depend, for its implementation, more upon an informal and always emergent organization of community members than upon the formally organized institutional sectors such as volunteer groups with zero history (Moore & Feldt, 1993). These groups are usually initiated to perform a service or task or to problem solve. Zero history groups have been formed so recently they have no history of operation and can many times move beyond the problem of the chronological planning trap.

This then provides some of the basis for our work with community groups. Action learning and action planning, the social planning action process, community development, and social process provide some of the foundation for our framework for community economic development work.

CHAPTER 2

Defining Community Economic Development

An important issue in our work with community groups is our strong feeling that an inordinate amount of time is spent debating what distinguishes community development from economic development. The debate is somewhat similar to the process versus content versus product question raised earlier (see Chapter 1) in that, among academic and professional practitioners, community development is seen as process-oriented and economic development as more content or outcome-oriented. We do not lightly dismiss these arguments but build our framework around a much more encompassing definition of what we call *community economic development*.

We argue that there is a direct relationship between economic development and community development that cannot be separated. In our view of community economic development, the whole is simply the sum of its parts. Economic development is a part of a larger, more important process involving and reflecting the life and activity of the total community. In our many years of work in community economic development we have noted that community leaders and officials all too often fail to look beyond the single event of recruiting a business or industry to the bigger picture of what does this recruitment ultimately mean to the community, to the quality of life of community residents, and to the long term future of a community and the surrounding area.

We concur with Holladay (1992, p. 38) when he emphasizes that there are few places that have put the community first and recognize that " . . . a quality economic development program is a manifestation of a quality community." We believe that how "quality communities" are attained relates most importantly to how and why communities go about involving local people representing all organizations and factions, especially women and minorities, in sum, all segments of the community in action learning and action planning. If factions or "segments" of people in a community economic development process are neglected then quality anything is not attainable.

Additionally, in our community economic development work we have increasingly noticed that "good" community organization structure reflects the "good" community development process and corresponding "good" economic result. That is, in our framework, how members of the community come together to discuss their strengths, weaknesses, and future directions, how they action learn and action plan, is critical to how they will organize their efforts for transforming their community economically.

Another important foundation for our definition of community economic development comes from the classic scholarship of community development. Christenson and Robinson (1980, p. 12) define community development as (1) a group of people (2) in a community (3) reaching a decision (4) to initiate a social action process (i.e., planned intervention) (5) to change (6) their economic, social, cultural, or environmental situation. We feel that community development must also involve and go beyond just reaching the decision—it must move toward action and follow-up. This is what we have implemented with selected communities during the past 5 years.

How do we define for people what our process, our framework, is all about? Several points come out in the community development literature and are summarized by Cary (1970). His analysis of the process provides us the elements that define our framework for working with groups:

1. Community, as represented and defined by the group, as the unit of action

2. Community initiative and leadership as resources

3. Use of both internal and external resources

4. Inclusive participation

5. An organized, comprehensive approach that attempts to involve the entire community

6. Community development as the objective of economic development or any community activity

7. Democratic, rational task accomplishment

These then become the basis for how community economic development groups begin to go about transforming their communities and how we facilitate our action planning process with community groups.

TRANSFORMATION IDEA

In the transformation of communities we see the need to extend Christenson and Robinson's (1980) definition to include implementation of social action and change. What takes place in the transformation then is the reflection and learning about community organization and change by participants. Discussion, reflection, and follow-up activities by the group are critical parts of the action learning process as conceived by Revans (1980). We see these elements as an integration of community development processes with economic development actions.

From our perspective, there is a continuing, recurring progression of activities that leads people through an action learning process or through a community and economic development undertaking. This recurring progression of activities goes beyond the Christenson and Robinson (1980) definition of community development. Our conception of action learning and community and economic development includes additional components that are best explained by the following model.

A WORKING MODEL

In our view all successful action learning or community economic development begins with some stimulus, or some disorienting dilemma (Mezirow, 1978). Individuals are constantly collecting input about their communities or disorienting dilemmas. This input is what we call in our model *data*. *Data* becomes "facts" or statistics, things we believe, or images about our environment, situation, or community. This *data* gets organized into *information*. *Information* is sets of data that help us identify and define a problem or issue in our environment, situation, or community. When we begin to put this information together we build *knowledge*. *Knowledge* is organized information that we begin to put together that helps us better define and outline problems and situations and potential solutions or methods for addressing these problems or issues. Once we organize knowledge we can begin to create *applications*. *Application* is using our organized knowledge to put actual solutions or action steps into process for addressing our problems or issues. *Implementation* becomes the important step of putting our applications to work, trying them out on our problems and issues. We then must continually *evaluate* what we are doing, or as we describe the process, ask the key questions through a dedicated effort of *follow-up*. When we ask key questions through a *follow-up* procedure we are collecting new *data* which moves us back into the process, or the recurring progression of activities that makes up our action learning/planning model (Figure 2.1).

We see our action learning/planning model as progressing beyond the Christenson and Robinson (1980) definition because we include implementation, evaluation, follow-up, and the continual recurring set of activities in our model as important parts of a definition that adequately captures the essence of action learning and community economic development.

This model provides the basis for community economic development groups to begin work. The disorienting dilemma, or ugly baby, gives community groups a focus or an orientation around which to begin. Overcoming inertia as it relates to disorienting dilemmas is an important first step toward action learning. Progressing through our model is the important next step. Continuing through the progression of activities in our working model is action learning and action planning.

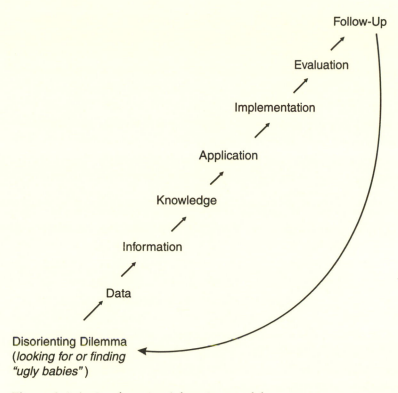

Follow-Up

Evaluation

Implementation

Application

Knowledge

Information

Data

Disorienting Dilemma
(*looking for or finding*
"ugly babies")

Figure 2.1 Action learning/planning model

Toward a Working Framework

The outline of our process for community economic development work with community groups has begun to take shape. Following Mezirow (1978): as a condition or dilemma develops; community members are concerned; they seek confirmation of the dilemma; and help in working on solutions. We add another dimension, provided by Whorton (1993), and Moore and Feldt (1993), who describe a bottom-up approach, which is our focus on democratic involvement, where individuals, with some convener and facilitator assistance, can form groups to work on common issues and problems.

Carnall (1990), Conner (1993), and Stewart (1991) view issues and dilemmas in organizations from a change management perspective. When workers, managers, and executives come together and share visions for a common objective, the resulting learning and empowerment process liberates groups to be creative and to transform their environments. Glance and Huberman (1994) suggest that as organizations and groups are restructured into smaller units, members may begin to feel more secure within the small group and tend to work toward collaborative solutions to social dilemmas.

Sanders (1966), Wilkinson (1991), and Nix (1977) outline procedures and techniques for bringing individuals together to work on shared concerns from a community organization and development perspective. The social action planning process approach engages individuals from different points of view and political orientations. Accommodating these different perspectives may take time, especially with the potential for conflict between different philosophies and problem-solving techniques. However, if the change or transformation is to be implemented in a specific community or organization, it is imperative to allocate time for discussion, questioning, modifications, and consensus building to develop action plans. The dialogue, discussion, clarification, and vision-sharing process is precisely the action learning process promoted by Revans (1980) and Freire (1968).

Our framework for communities to change (see Figure 2.2) themselves involves community action, community development, economic development, action learning, perspective transformation, and action planning, with implementation, follow-up, and reflection to ask new questions. We see these concepts and strategies coming together in a transformative bottom-up process that forms the basis for this presentation.

A Suggested Framework

- A social dilemma, problem, or issue confronts individuals who share this information and realize that several people may be concerned and they may also have many different perceptions for solving the problem.

Figure 2.2 Framework for community economic development

- Individuals or a small group may discuss the issues or dilemma and suggest they seek assistance from a larger group, experts, resource persons, group process persons such as facilitators, or other sources.
- Groups tend to move into two general patterns (with many variations): A *top-down and directive approach* to problem solving where experts tell the group how to respond and what to do and another approach, supported by Mezirow (1978), Freire (1968), Gaventa (1980), and others, called *bottom-up* where the group empowers itself and learns about change and social actions.
- Learning and skill development are promoted in the bottom-up approach regarding small group process, conflict resolu-

tion, community organization, empowerment, small group decision making and problem solving, social action, and change management.

- Transforming communities need support from trained professionals, volunteers, elected public officials, and the business community to identify ideas and put plans into action.
- Most communities need mechanisms for generating economic and quality of life benefits to residents (e.g., employment, recreation, education, spiritual support, protection, housing, and public assistance).
- Economic development alternatives are generated from perspectives of participants, actions of individuals and groups from other communities, support from statewide economic developers, and the examples of successful economic development strategies in other states or regions.
- Community development actions similar to those cited by Freire (1968), Gaventa (1980), Revans (1980), and others emphasize participant involvement, empowerment, and continuous learning.
- Action planning is done by local citizens and participants in community economic development programs. It involves a shared vision of the community; change or transformation; understanding and willingness of participants to risk change; focusing attention on what needs to change; accepting responsibility for beginning the transformation process; committing time, energy, and effort to work on identified events or projects; reporting back to the community group or organization the progress or problems involved in risking change; making adaptations where needed to the action plans; and proceeding with agreed upon group projects.

SUMMARY

The framework we outline in Chapter 1 and the definition we propose in Chapter 2 are the basis, or foundation, for implementing community economic development in our perspective. The following chapters discuss details and provide examples of how communities and groups are action planning and making changes to encourage community economic development. These ideas and examples are not mutually exclusive or exhaustive, but they do represent illustrative applications of selected theories and concepts outlined in our working model of community economic development.

CHAPTER 3

Educating, Training, and Organizing Community Volunteers

How many times have you heard community economic development groups say, "The key to our success will be getting *educated* to do a better job of community economic development"? How many times have you also heard, at meetings and seminars you have attended on community economic development, the speakers and seminar leaders promote "get *training* on this or that economic development subject before you begin to make changes in your community"? At other economic development meetings you have no doubt seen and heard presenters promote the theme of "get your community organized!" The implied promise of all these meetings and their presenters is that education, training, and organization are the magic bullets for ensuring community economic development success. Whom do you believe? Which course, from among education, training, and organizing, do you take first? Are they different or are they the same? How can you possibly get educated, trained, organized, and do all of the things you know or think ought to be done in order to make incremental and even lasting changes in your community?

THE DIFFERENCE BETWEEN
EDUCATION AND TRAINING

We advocate the belief that there is a difference between education and training. This is our premise and it is based upon our work with hundreds of community groups over the past 20 years. Education in community economic development situations is the process of individuals or community groups learning about their current need or dilemma. There may be more than one appropriate and possible solution to the need or dilemma. The process of what and how people learn about identifying, testing out, and revising these alternative solutions is action learning and an educational process.

Education is the process in our loop, of moving from data to information to knowledge (see Figure 2.1 in Chapter 2). Training is designed for a specific and much narrower context. Nadler (1984) makes a distinction between education, training, and development. We go beyond Nadler by taking the position that training is a much narrower concept than education.

We see education as a lifelong process whereas training is time specific for a particular need or problem. For example, a community group may have difficulty understanding and utilizing demographic data to promote the economic potential of their area. There is a need for the group to be educated about the availability of demographic data, how data can assist them in "telling their community story," and how this information is also useful for preparing applications for funding from various agencies and foundations. Someone in the group, or the entire group, may need training in using the technology (i.e., computers and computer programs) to locate, retrieve, and display the data in tables and charts to assist in telling the community story.

We believe education is the process for learning about the concept or issue, posing options or alternatives, testing out possible solutions (trial and error), and revising options for applications in the community. Training would be helpful, in the above example, to develop specific skills (e.g., computer generated data displays) to assist in achieving the overall objective of the group, that is, to present their community story with data displays.

Confusion about Training

We believe that all too often economic developers, especially those in professional, full-time roles in the community, confuse training with education. The suggestion is often made to have the group "trained" to do a better job of economic development. We see this as the "quick fix syndrome" of community economic development. Since many community economic development efforts are time driven, they fall into the problems outlined in the planning trap (see Figure 1.1 in Chapter 1). Training becomes a quick fix to address the community economic development problem or dilemma.

However, based on our experience, we maintain that a different approach, the undertaking of the action learning/planning model we propose in Chapter 2, is a much more valuable technique. Community volunteer groups, through the application of the process outlined in our action learning/planning model and through the action learning process, set out to gather information, knowledge, and results and have them presented in an educational format. We emphasize the range and scope of the issue and the many creative ways the group could devise strategies for solving the problem or overcoming the dilemma. At a later time during this action learning/planning process, it may be appropriate for someone to be trained to perform services for the group (as a grant writer for example, to assist the group in presenting their story to a funding agency). In this example, the grant writer would help the group apply the information and knowledge they have acquired about their community to seek support in making needed changes or improvements.

Problem Solving

The important distinction between training and education, especially as it relates to volunteer groups engaged in community economic development, is that education about community economic development is a broader examination of many options that may be useful for problem solving, change, or improvements in the community. In contrast, training is acquiring a specific skill to answer a particular question. Both activities are important to community economic development, but education may be the place to start with the community group before selecting specific skills (e.g., data analysis or grant writing) that may be required to assist in the educational problem solving process.

Our intent in this chapter is to offer some suggestions for working with community groups regarding education, training, and community organization. We do not recommend that one activity must absolutely happen before others, or that the activities are mutually exclusive, but there are some general recommendations for which activity to start on first. What we have done in this chapter is organized our comments and examples as the chapter title suggests: educating, training, and organizing community volunteers.

EDUCATING COMMUNITY VOLUNTEERS

Elected officials, community leaders, volunteers, and local residents can all benefit from learning about their community. What are the basic descriptive statistics (population, employment, formal education completed by residents, number and type of employers, products and services located in the area) about their community and how does this data compare with nearby counties, cities, communities, or regions? How does the community compare with other areas in the state or region? Some of this data can be obtained from chambers of commerce, state agencies, and data/forecasting offices at state or regional universities.

Various data, in the form of statistics, are readily available on many different components or variables that can and do affect the economic indicators and quality of life in communities. How these data are obtained, understood, and used for problem solving (the application and implementation in our action learning/planning model) is the educational or learning project dimension of community economic development. Numbers exist on almost any factor you can imagine but only become important and useful in the context of a specific question or resolution to a controversy. The number 42.9%, for example, has no meaning until it is explained that this is the high school dropout rate for students attending a given school.

There are a variety of ways to become educated about your community. When we work with community or regional groups we try not to embarrass group members by saying they are uneducated or misinformed about the community or area they live in. What we try to do in a light-hearted and humorous way is suggest we all play a trivia game about the community on an individual basis and then share and discuss our answers in small groups. This becomes the way we can promote discussion in the larger group about what we collectively know and do not know about the community.

The point of the trivia game is to raise awareness about many types of information that we take for granted or, more importantly, wrongly assume we know. The discussion continues with what variables and factors we should know about, and how to find up-to-date information about community conditions that we may not know about (e.g., educational levels, family income, teenage pregnancies, etc.). These factors could have an impact on how the community may change, and consequently improve the economic opportunities for its residents.

When working with community or regional groups, we often ask them to gather their own information and data for problem solving. We assist them in discussing, clarifying, and defining the problem or dilemma. Once this is accomplished we ask the group what information or data they need to document the situation. We assist them in designing a survey tool, such as a questionnaire, interview guide, or observation instrument, and suggesting which individuals or groups would be candidates for completing or responding to the survey. The group must know the following before gathering the first response:

- The problem
- The questions to ask
- The people that need to reply
- The ways of summarizing the survey results

TRIVIA GAME

We select our information or data from the U.S. Census, Georgia Interactive Atlas, or other published data sources for a community, region, or state. We may even obtain information published by the local chamber of commerce to help us in designing the game.

1. What is your location's (city, county, region, etc.) population?
2. How many in your location dropped out of high school last year?
3. How many people are employed in your location?
4. How many people, employed in your location, reside outside of your county (or city)?
5. How many new businesses were started in your location last year?
6. How many existing businesses expanded their operations (by creating new jobs) in your location last year?
7. How many people over age 25 that reside in your location have completed high school or college?
8. Can you name the state or federal parks and national forests in your location?
9. Can you name 5 of the 10 historical sites in your location?
10. Can you name 5 of the 25 churches or synagogues or mosques in your location?
11. Are there any protected natural areas in your location (e.g., marshes or swamps or sites)?
12. What types of public cable access or international telecommunications systems are available in your location?
13. How many miles of paved and unpaved county-maintained roads are there in your location?
14. How many public housing units are there in your location?
15. How many public-maintained recreation sites are there in your location?

The action learning project (i.e., educational objective) is for the group to discuss their perceptions of the controversy or dilemma and to work together using problem-solving and decision-making processes to inform themselves, to learn about the issue, and to use their fact finding to assist in posing and selecting possible alternative options for a solution. What they gain in learning about issues, facts, perceptions, and group processes enables them to pose new, more difficult, and precise problems. Sometimes the frustrations in identifying the precise problem or dilemma and the misinformation about what options are available to solve the problem are too great and the group may quit or become embroiled in conflict and controversy or may disband altogether. All of these are potential products of learning about and doing community economic development.

Leaders of the action learning/planning process can emerge from the local group itself, or they can be secured from "outside" the community from agencies or organizations, such as state agencies, universities, and the private sector (i.e., business or industry). Consultants may also be recruited to assist the group to examine their situation and to assist the group in developing an action learning strategy to work on local issues. In our view, it really doesn't matter where the catalyst or leaders for change and action learning come from as long as they emerge or can be brought into the process. Education then is the sum total of activities, processes, analyses, reflection, and hard work that individuals share with each other and the group to make difficult decisions and to problem solve for change in the community.

Examples of the Education Process

Two real communities, designated as A and B, are described in the following examples. Community A worked hard and educated themselves but did not involve other volunteers in the education process. On the other hand, Community B invested their time and energies in educating a broader base of volunteers which produced a longer-lasting effort.

Community A

Community A worked with a small group of people (5 or 6) to develop and learn about community economic development. The dynamic leader and a few hard-working individuals took it upon themselves to educate themselves to learn about economic development. They tried very hard to recruit others in their learning efforts and were not successful. In frustration they moved ahead on their own. Community residents observed this and let them do all the work and make all the decisions. Most of the community residents were very passive in their support of the changes. They liked them but they were the work of X group or that one person.

Community A was successful in cleaning up the downtown area, repainting signs, engaging merchants in clean up, renovating old buildings, and securing new business downtown. However, most of the changes in the community were attributed to the leader and a small group of supporters. After 18 months the leader burned out and was frustrated because of having to "do it all myself." The small support group also burned out and unfortunately, no other supporters had been recruited to carry on with the community projects.

Community B

In contrast, Community B had a tradition of involving and educating several agency boards composing an active group of 25 to 30 community residents, leaders, and elected officials. Community meetings were held with many of the different boards/agencies represented. People, groups, and boards were informed of the need for community economic development activities. Past successes of multiple groups working on priority projects were the catalysts and motivators for working on new action agenda items. Elected officials, local leaders, and residents in the community made certain that community members were informed and that successors to elected or appointed positions were brought into the problem-solving and decision-making processes. Educating the broader community and successors has been the basis upon which Community B has identified and accomplished priority projects for community economic development and change.

Outcomes of the Education Process

What are the outcomes from an educational approach to community economic development? These factors are not identified in any order or priority but are cited so that the reader will be informed and aware of them. In all instances the time involved to accomplish these activities depends upon the local situation and the commitment of those involved to get the job done. However, several elements must be present for communities to be successful in promoting community economic development:

- Keeping an open mind for change and development
- Having the ability to share information with the community, including both those who support and may not support the ideas or issues under discussion
- Listening and adjusting to many different voices and suggestions for change
- Continuously seeking more people to get involved and taking on both large and small tasks related to accomplishing the overall goal or vision
- Taking time to review and reflect with leaders, elected officials, and residents the projects and directions supported by the larger group
- Promoting the accomplishment of the task as a community or group project with many sharing the credit and acclaim
- Accepting that controversy and conflict will be encountered on most, if not all, projects that affect many people in the community
- Having an overall vision or goal, supported by the larger community, to work toward achieving; something that a large majority of community members can support
- Continuing to expand the view of the community to work

toward single projects while not losing site of long-range objectives or visions
- Taking time to reflect and celebrate what has been accomplished in the community; special events to draw attention to
completed projects and tasks
- Being persistent and making sure others are informed of what
has been suggested, accomplished, and yet to be completed

TRAINING COMMUNITY VOLUNTEERS

To do any job or task or fulfill specific responsibilities, we
may need training! Training for some is a narrowly applied set
of experiences designed to specify and reinforce certain behav-
iors. In this narrow context, examples of these trainable skills
could be identified as community data analyses, fund raising
approaches, or locating an industrial park, and many more
specific tasks that are often related to the larger context of developing community economic potentials.

We want to get beyond the narrow view to a more comprehensive perception of training. Examples of so-called training
opportunities for economic development are really educational
programs such as those offered through AEDC (American Economic Development Council) sponsored programs at the University of Oklahoma (EDI) and at Georgia Tech (the Basic Economic Development Institute). Opportunities for combining
community development skills with economic development
are offered at the University of Georgia CEDP, at the Heartland
Center in Lincoln, Nebraska, and at the Community Development Institute at the Winrock Center in Conway, Arkansas.

A recent endeavor in Georgia by the Governor's Development Council (GDC) is the Georgia Academy for Economic Development, which is an in-state, regionally-based training effort
to inform groups about economic development. Elected public
officials, community leaders, and volunteers *learn* about apply-
ing community economic development to a multi-county region
and learn about and designate an action plan for implementation.

The desired outcome of these programs from the many

different states and economic development organizations is education for the human capital development (Schultz, 1961; Becker, 1975) of citizens and community leaders to understand and be willing to take on specific projects or efforts to preserve, change, or develop the community for both economic and quality of life benefits.

About Training

Our point is that if specific skills are sliced and diced into small manageable units for training, then the individual is hard pressed to find help or to learn on his or her own time to put all of these pieces together to make them add up to community economic development.

For example, you can gather information and data about which baby boomers have money, like to travel, and would come to your community as visitors or tourists; but how does this fit into an overall strategy of marketing historic, recreation, and potential tourism sites in your community for economic development? This information and data needs to be plugged into an overall discussion and plan for attracting, accommodating, and encouraging overnight and repeat visits to your community recreation and historic sites, while at the same time protecting them from overuse.

Attending to these issues is a broader perspective and it involves educating ourselves about the long-term implications of utilizing information and data that we have been trained to acquire. We are proposing that communities adopt a broader approach to learning about community economic development and then seek the specific skills they need.

ORGANIZING COMMUNITY VOLUNTEERS

"Next week I'm going to get organized!" The time is now! Volunteers in the community are usually available but not for an unlimited period of time. Claire Cline (1984), a volunteer coordinator with whom we have worked, maintains that to succeed in community development endeavors you must treat volunteers like staff. That is, ask them to perform specific tasks within a specified time frame. Volunteers will control their time about when and where they can perform the work. The organizer or organizing agency's role is to identify and clarify tasks and make the tasks fit within the volunteers' time frame.

How are these roles preformed by the organizer/organizing agency? The process employed by the organizer is to help the problem-solving and decision-making group to clearly describe and define the dilemma and the many options available to help solve the problem. The following example shows an issue that has been clarified:

> We need to support the development and siting in the region of a recycling solid waste facility that will serve the six surrounding counties and other interested communities, on a first come first served basis, with a guaranteed tonnage of _____ for _____ years until _____ (date).

Community volunteers, individuals, and groups can clearly read the issue. What is the basis for the statement and the need? The issue can be presented to many different groups in the community for discussion, information and data gathering, analysis of findings, and presentation of results to the taxpayers in the community. A cross section of the community could address this dilemma and allocate volunteers and community members to various tasks, such as designing surveys (i.e., developing information gathering tools), actual information gathering, information analysis, reporting, presenting information, and publicity. Assignments could be made by group, talent, skill, special interest, or a host of other mechanisms. The important concern to keep in mind is representation across the community and making the tasks fit in terms of scope and intensity, for volunteers.

Organizing community groups and volunteers is both *art* and *science*. The art involves many variables, such as safeguarding egos, cultural differences, and political agendas, while not compromising the process of information gathering and reporting. From the science viewpoint, organizers and organizing agencies must be adept at designing, conducting, and carrying out tasks and enabling the group to learn what and why they did each step in the action learning/planning process.

Carver (1990) suggests that communities can redesign themselves in the way they organize and communicate within and between nonprofit boards or community agencies. Conner (1993) proposes that leaders can involve others in "managing at the speed of change" by giving them the tools to do the work they decide is important to the organization. Sanders (1966) and Warren (1978) suggest analyzing and using the existing social structure of communities or organizations to communicate what is the "desired change" and making sure that the community culture is not abridged. We are drawing from the above sources, as well as others (Revans, 1980; Freire, 1968; and Mezirow, 1978) to propose the framework for action learning that combines problem solving, decision making, and action learning skills into the community organization process.

Specifically, we have encouraged communities to organize themselves using these guidelines:

1. Discuss the idea or issue with several different groups: elected officials, community leaders, community civic groups, a cross section of the religious community, and business and industry leaders or managers. Are they in general agreement about the need to *do something*? They may have no answers or may offer many different ideas for solution.

2. Ask a broad cross section (say 25 to 40 persons) of the community to agree to devote at least 8 hours, or better yet, an entire weekend to discussing the issue.

3. Engage facilitators, community economic developers, and community change specialists in working with a planning or steering committee of the larger group to design a meeting to explore the issue or issues.

4. Hold the meeting; see what emerges as issues, dilemmas, or challenges.

5. Obtain commitments from participants attending the meeting (plus others) to continue to explore the issues and to work toward finding or making up new options for solving problems or issues.

6. Design an action plan with opportunities for participants, represented agencies, and other interested groups to take part in implementing the action plans.

7. Have each person and group involved accept responsibility for communicating and clarifying what the action plans are and how the entire community will benefit from their accomplishment.

8. Specify the dates and locations for when and where the group will get together to report on accomplishments, trials, errors, and need for readjusting the action plans.

9. Have each person and group involved accept responsibility for communicating and clarifying specific *parts* of the action plans and how the entire community will benefit from their accomplishment.

10. Set aside time to update the action plan.

11. Don't forget to designate a date, time, and place for the community to celebrate action plan accomplishments.

Hopefully, we have outlined for you our designation of the differences between and importance of education, training, and organization as it relates to community economic development. From our experience, any effort that takes an educational approach to problem solving and decision making will have a better chance of success in your community.

TIPS FOR EDUCATING, TRAINING, AND ORGANIZING COMMUNITY GROUPS

1. Listen to individuals and community groups as they identify issues or problems.
2. Bring together a cross section of the community to discuss shared concerns.
3. Use facilitated meeting techniques to capture what people say. Provide reports, both written and visual history, of group meetings to the larger community.
4. Ask for volunteers to work on activities or projects selected as important by the group.
5. Provide a support mechanism or process for keeping the group and community informed of progress and the need for more volunteers to help out.
6. Share the work and rewards with represented groups and the community.
7. Plan ahead; add new activities to the "to do" list or action plan.

CHAPTER 4

Preserving Environmentally Sensitive and Historic Areas

Every community should view their historic and natural resources as special commodities that should be preserved and protected. Environmentally sensitive areas can generate vocal supporters both pro and con and lead to potentially contentious situations. However, from a community economic development standpoint, it is necessary to be very aware of environmentally sensitive areas; of the economic development implications they hold for a community; and of the legal parameters that define, preserve, and protect them. All too often, this is the one area that can entangle your community in a "growth" versus "no-growth" situation.

Does this necessarily have to happen? Most people are likely to equate the environmental movement and those that advocate it as antigrowth (Sills, 1975). At the same time, it is important to realize that most people also support community economic development activities (Maurer & Christenson, 1982). Do these activities have to be in juxtaposition to each other? Our experience in working with these matters with community groups tells us the answer is "no." A number of people believe that communities can both support economic development activities and preserve and protect the community environment at the same time (Willits, Crider & Janota, 1993).

WATER

Perhaps the most precious resource for any community is its water supply, streams, rivers, and marshlands. These are all environmentally sensitive areas that need to be preserved and protected as an area changes and develops. A community is like a living organism. Water is the resource a community depends upon for its survival. Whether water is used for drinking, industrial processing, wastewater, recreation, or irrigation, it is indispensable for community growth and survivability.

Everybody lives downstream! If we live by this motto then we need to consider what we take out of our water resources and what we put back into them. Communities can have environmental quality and development, if they will recognize the importance of this resource and plan wisely. We know a public service commissioner in Georgia who says that many water quality problems could be solved by making communities put their intake pipes downstream of their wastewater outlet.

Water is a resource that has many economic development potentials. In some instances a water resource, such as a river, can be an economic development generator as a white-water rafting, canoeing, and/or tubing site. Communities in areas nearby trout fishing streams know the volume of business that is generated when trout season is in full swing. The key to how economically viable the water can remain relates to how much disturbance people, both buyers and sellers, will make when they use the site and in what condition they will maintain the site.

A study conducted at the University of Georgia (McNamara & Kriesel, 1990) tried to find those correlates that made communities attractive to retirees. The findings of that study indicated that the amount of elevation change and surface acres of water present were the factors that correlated most highly with areas that attracted large numbers of retirees. You can see that mountain communities on lakes or with rivers will be successful at attracting retirees. Most importantly, water, whether lakes, rivers, or the ocean, is an important lure for retirees.

Water is a magnet for people in this country and always has been. Look at the history of the development of cities in this country that are located on major rivers or the coast. Water, whether used for recreation, consumption, industrial processing, or irrigation, is critical to economic development.

WETLANDS

Communities that are fortunate enough to have marshland, like the Everglades in Florida, the Great Dismal Swamp in Virginia, and the Okefenokee Swamp in Georgia, are probably not in the mosquito growing business but they could access or promote the marsh as a site for nature photography, nature walks, ecosystem tours, or bird watching. Marshlands and wetlands provide ideal nesting sites for birds and support an abundant assortment of wildlife.

Near Grand Island, Nebraska, preservationists, conservationists, and wildlife protectors have raised their voices to protest the possible damming of the Platte River. Why? Because this is a resting and nesting area for the sandhill crane. This beautiful creature needs shallow water for resting, nearby cornfields for feeding, and sandbars for doing "what comes naturally" during the course of their mating dance. If the river was ever dammed or altered in any way it is doubtful that the sandhill crane would survive. Rather than let this environmentally sensitive area be a barrier to community economic development, local leaders, artists, landowners, and conservationists have worked individually and together to protect the river, sand bars, water quality, and birds and at the same time have promoted this region as an economic asset.

The Okefenokee Swamp, near Waycross, Georgia, is promoted as the "land of the trembling earth." The swamp is home to a multitude of wild creatures and plant species including birds, alligators, fish, aquatic plants, wildflowers, and trees. An example of protecting environmentally sensitive areas and local culture is the enterprising entrepreneur who rebuilt the home site of an original *swamper* and gave it the name of Obediah's Okefenokee. This is an excellent case study of an economic development project that started at ground zero and is now slowly building a reputation as a tourist attraction. Obediah's includes an elevated walkway in the swamp, a restored farmstead, gardens, wildlife exhibit, and museum and diorama of artifacts and life in the swamp during the late 1800s and early 1900s. All it took was an idea, sweat equity, patience, and persistence.

HISTORIC LAND, EVENTS, AND SITES

Many communities are fortunate to have historic sites, events, and structures that add character to the area. As a nation, we are beginning to value our heritage and to draw attention to unique areas, events, and sites by erecting markers or monuments for residents and visitors to appreciate. As more international visitors come to the United States, we need to improve our signage as it relates to tourism destinations. We encourage communities to take a lesson from the signs found in national parks and create unique local signs that incorporate important information in a concise and attractive manner.

Some communities, for example Crawfordville in Taliaferro County, Georgia, have taken inventory of their downtown buildings and more recently of the homes in town. A historic preservation class from the University of Georgia, under the supervision of Professor John Waters, conducted an inventory of the homes in Crawfordville and classified each building by date of construction, type of architecture, building materials, and design. This inventory was presented to community leaders and placed on file at the community library for future use in preservation and planning. It is interesting to note that downtown Crawfordville has been used for eight movies and over twenty television shows. When we have facilitated community meetings in Crawfordville and worked with local community groups, one of their goals has been (and is) to preserve the downtown as a viable area and as a working movie set. Storefronts and streets are preserved with the 1940s through 1950s themes and they intend to keep the town in this condition in hopes of recruiting other film makers and television producers.

Other communities have the benefit of being a river community, much like St. Louis, Missouri, which is on the Mississippi River; and Maysville, Kentucky, which is on the Ohio River in northeast Kentucky. Individual owners along the rivers have restored homes, row houses, and stores to promote tourism and the feeling of times-gone-by from the 1940s or 1950s. Augusta and Columbus, Georgia, have built new "river walks" along the Savannah and Chattahoochee Rivers respectively. Augusta's river walk is connected with sidewalks to nearby hotels where patrons or conventioneers can enjoy the scenic beauty after a long day in meetings. Columbus has connected its river walk to the convention center and other shops in the historic downtown area. One of the local attractions near the river walk in Columbus is the historic Springer Hotel and Opera House, which has been renovated to include a piano bar for people to visit after they attend plays or concerts at the Opera House.

One individual who retired from the U.S. Postal Service in Savannah, Georgia, did not retire from helping friends and neighbors to preserve their heritage, culture, and homes. Mr. W. W. Law who "carried the mail" in Savannah for over 25 years, saw on a daily basis the unique natural resources of an African-American community in this town. He became instrumental in recognizing the unique historical significance of the community and cautioned neighbors about making drastic structural changes to their homes and buildings. He worked with community leaders to establish a small museum that highlights the heritage and culture of the local people.

There are numerous groups that are interested in local history, especially as it is expressed in buildings and historical sites. Several years ago one of the authors was contacted by a preservationist group interested in locating old grist mill sites in Georgia. He was intrigued to find an entire organization, with an excellent magazine, that is interested in finding and preserving mill sites. This organization catalogs and provides a listing of sites, through their magazine, to members who like to travel and visit grist mill sites. We often encourage groups to think of historical sites beyond the traditional notions that usually asso-

ciate sites with political events or military occurrences. Many
communities overlook sites that may be associated with unique
local industry; educational institutions; specialized agriculture
and agricultural processing; forest products processing, or cul-
tivation practices; mining; indigenous crafts; folk art; or religious practices or sects. Any or all of these may exist in a community and may well have significant economic development
potential. This requires thinking of your community outside
your traditional paradigm or model.

HOW TO GET STARTED IN
IDENTIFYING AND PRESERVING SITES

If you don't already know about identifying and preserving natural and historic sites and buildings in your community,
get a group together and start an inventory. Better still, take
several people on tours of the community, area, or region and
record unique water, land, structures, events, burial sites, and
unusual flora and fauna on paper as well as by photograph or
video. It may be helpful to contact a local office of the state
historical society, a college or university, the regional planning
agency, and older residents in the area to help with the inventory. If possible, hold hearings or meetings in the various communities to take *testimony* or gather firsthand accounts of
unique features that should be noted and preserved in the area.
From the hearings, listings, inventories, and photographs,
compile a composite of all the findings: wells, springs, streams,
rivers, land features, structures, events, battlefields, dwellings,
indigenous or unique plants and animals, etc. A good idea is to
use either a high school class or local civic club to put together
an *oral history* project of the area. Get on video if possible,
audio tape at the least, interviews with long-time residents who
can relate stories about local resources, including history, natural disasters, important events, and changes that have occurred
with local natural resources.
Check with local and regional planning agencies to see if

some of the buildings or sites qualify for designation on the National Register of Historic Sites or Locations. Also, check with state, regional, and local environmental agencies (e.g., Department of Natural Resources, Environmental Protection Agency) to see if some of the natural areas are subject to federal and state environmental regulations (e.g., wetlands law, endangered species law, and land use laws).

Review the list with preservation experts to see which areas or sites are subject to restrictions and regulations. Some of the areas may have potential for promotion as tourist vistas or photographic venues or areas for preservation development.

If your community has one or more sites with visitor or tourist potential, it would be helpful to make sure the area is protected from abuse by walkers, motor vehicles, air transportation, or boats. Also, make sure that the area is not overused by people needing food and restroom facilities.

The manner in which the community markets and promotes the sites is critical. Visitors tend to act differently if the site is advertised as a natural area accessible for educational and research purposes versus a site that has few or no restrictions.

EXAMPLE: DETERMINING WHAT TO PROTECT IN AN ENVIRONMENTALLY SENSITIVE AREA

Background

One of the requirements of the 1989 Georgia Planning Act is the designation and specification of Regionally Important Resources (RIRs). Three areas in the state have received preliminary designation as RIRs: the Augusta Canal, Pine Mountain Ridge, and the major river systems and related drainage areas in the state.

The 1989 Georgia Planning Law permits RIRs to be identified, described, and delineated. The legislation requires that resrouce management plans be developed to guide future uses within the RIR boundaries. These plans are required to have citizen involvement and to be presented for review by regional and state planning agencies (e.g., Regional Development Commissions, Department of Natural Resources, Department of Community Affairs, and any other agency with an interest in the area).

Citizen Involvement Regarding Pine Mountain

ICAD had a contract with the Department of Community Affairs (DCA) to facilitate community involvement and citizen participation in the discussion and delineation of planning factors related to the Pine Mountain area. The Pine Mountain Ridge and related area ("complex") is located in east central Georgia near the town of Warm Springs and encompasses several counties, small towns, and communities. To work on a management plan for regionally important resources, the recommended action was to involve citizens and elected officials from all of the towns, cities, counties, regional development commissions (RDCs), and other local and state agencies with expertise related to the region.

ICAD faculty (Susan Crow and associates) designed a series of activities that included the use of facilitated meeting strategies and disposable cameras. The Pine Mountain Group, a group selected to represent the region through an involved nomination process, elected to provide news releases to local media about purpose, activities, and results of the planning process.

The group of about 40 people was divided into small teams of 3 to 6 members. Each small group self-selected a route from among seven different travel routes, which included areas they would visit and photograph. The routes were determined in advance by ICAD staff based on information obtained during interviews with committee members. Routes were designated by themes such as the Cove, Highway 190 Scenic Byway, and the Presidential Route.

Pictures as a Way to Specify
Importance and Aesthetic Value

The task of the small groups was to travel along the designated routes, roadways, and trails in the area and take pictures of what they felt were important features, resources, and things to protect. They also took pictures of what they thought was undesirable in the area such as trash, abandoned automobiles, and visual clutter of signs. Each small group was given two 12-exposure cameras. They were instructed to discuss and select sites such as views, structures, scenic beauty, or areas needing cleanup/fix up for photographs. Photos were not consensus shots because any member could take any desired photo, but selecting the sites did stimulate a lot of discussion about "what is important and why." The trips took one entire day and generated over 100 photographs for discussion.

Each group presented some of their photos to the larger group. Small 2 X 3 inch photos were placed on an opaque projector and displayed on the wall for all in the group to see. Reactions were solicited from the larger group on such things as "What was the subject of the photo?", "Why was this photo taken?", and "What does this photo mean to you?"

Then the group presenting the photo was asked to comment on the same questions and discuss their purposes for taking the photos. Facilitators took notes and comments from all of the discussions by the large group. Facilitators asked the group to identify issues and regional planning themes such as site development, protection, improvements, clean-up/fix-up, and related concerns.

Because the photo experience was so well received and generated so many issues, reactions, and concerns, the ICAD team leader provided additional cameras for residents to take additional photos and present them at later meetings. There was interest among the committee for displaying photos and map routes at the regional library and regional planning agency for viewing by interested residents in the area.

Subsequent meetings included the reexamination of photos, confirmation of issues and concerns, and detailed discussions of elements that should be included in a management plan for the Pine Mountain Ridge area. It must be pointed out that at the second meeting of the Pine Mountain Group, there was sentiment for designating only the Pine Mountain State Park acreage as the designated area for the plan. As the group continued to meet and discuss, they appointed a subcommittee of the group to present several options for RIR boundary consideration which included the Pine Mountain Ridge, extensions of the ridge, and the viewsheds north and south of the ridge. This was an important element of the group process, which illustrates the ebb and flow of viewpoints. The Pine Mountain Ridge RIR has been expanded to include the watershed between Pine and Oak Mountains, and a corridor along a portion of the Flint River.

Follow-up

After the Pine Mountain Ridge complex had been defined, described, delineated, and specified, a detailed plan was prepared and submitted for state level review. The DCA Board reviews the Resource Management Strategy (RMS) and gives final designation to the area. The Resource Management Plan (RMP) will guide planning decisions within the RIR area. Each year the group will need to review and update the document based on the 1989 Georgia Planning Act as they see the need resulting from implementation of the RIR plan.

Benefits Associated with Using Cameras

The following comments by Susan Crow, ICAD team leader, illustrate the benefits associated with using cameras as a tool for citizen involvement:

• People got to know each other quickly and learned about the region from each other. There was a lot of discussion about sites to photograph, both positive and negative.

- Cameras generated active participation by all of the people in each of the vans as they drove their self-selected routes through the area. Crow provided route maps for the area so that the entire Pine Mountain Ridge complex was travelled by one or more vans.
- Local folks became recognized experts. We found out that local people really do know a lot about where they live and what they want to protect.
- Participants saw resources from very different perspectives; for example, what some people viewed as positives (e.g., billboards and signs) others viewed as negatives. Selecting sites to photograph generated much discussion about why and what was being presented as a valued or important environmental feature.
- As they viewed the photos, issues about important features and distracting views came out quickly in the group discussions. The photos made the distinctions between views very clear.
- Photos can be used again for exhibits and as an historical perspective or record of what the group did to identify and select important features in the RIR area.

ECONOMIC BENEFITS TO THE COMMUNITY

Historic sites and natural areas can be one of the many features of a community or town. There are few locations that derive all of their support from historic or natural areas. Williamsburg, Virginia is a community that uses its historic village as the sole focus for economic development. Hotels, motels, restaurants, and services have located near Williamsburg to provide visitors with the services to stay for several days. Yellowstone National Park in Wyoming is one of the few natural areas that derives most of its economic benefits from visitors in the summer and snowmobilers or cross-country skiers in the winter. For most communities, a historic building or Native American burial ground or natural area will be one of several attractions to the community or region. Also, a given site will attract people with different interests related to the specific area. For example, hikers, bikers, and campers may be interested in a park or forest area. Lakes and streams in the area may invite recreational fishing. Runners, walkers, and health enthusiasts may be able to use some of the same facilities as hikers, bikers, and campers. However, a historic hotel with lodging, restaurant, and meeting facilities in a community may attract many different kinds of visitors such as those on bus tours, scenic tours, elderhostels, educational tours, or business and industry groups. Historic battlefields, burial grounds, and unique land features such as high cliffs or marshes may attract still another type of visitor who may have different needs for food, lodging, and services.

If your community is small and has only one or two unique features that might attract visitors, then team up with nearby communities to promote their attractions as well. In several southern states there is a Highway 27 Historic Court House Tour that has proved to be successful in drawing people into an entire region. The tour promotes old and historic court houses along a single highway where communities can display their buildings, promote local crafts and products, and possibly offer lodging or food services at the end of the traveller's day.

Three communities in central Georgia got an idea for an "antique trail" from their visits in Iowa where several communities displayed and sold antiques and promoted other stores in nearby towns. People searching for antiques will go a long way to find what they want. Each community promoted others on the antique trail in the region and also offered information about store hours, items for sale, and phone numbers to call for specific information. Regional planning agencies in some states have historic developer/planners on their staff, who can assist in inventorying and evaluating historic sites, locating craftspeople for renovations, and helping community leaders with applications for National Historic Register status.

TIPS FOR PRESERVING HISTORIC
AND SCENIC AREAS

1. Conduct an inventory of the unique historic, scenic, and environmentally sensitive areas in your community; also inventory nearby and adjoining sites.
2. Determine which sites are currently available or could be developed and preserved for public access.
3. Determine which sites meet federal, state, or local standards or requirements for preservation designation and/or funding for preservation.
4. Interview visitors: Why do they visit? What have they learned? What additional information or services do they need? Would they come back for a repeat visit? Would they recommend the site to others? Why? Why not?
5. Check out the possibility of promoting historic sites, scenic beauty, and sensitive environmental areas as topics or subjects in elderhostel programs or community institutes promoted by local universities or community schools.

CHAPTER 5

Revitalizing the Community and Downtown Areas

Downtown. What images come to mind when you think of your community's downtown? Is it a retail center? A commercial center? A concentration of professional services and government offices? Do you see your downtown as dying or on the ropes? Maybe you conjure up a picture of the downtown as the center of the community, typified perhaps by a town square, government buildings, department stores, and parks. A romantic vision perhaps, but a realistic portrait of what downtown is, or was, in many cases. However, from a community economic development perspective, more important questions might be, "What images does your community's downtown convey to others who might be passing through?" and "How do others in your community view the role and possibilities of downtown in a total community economic development scheme?" To our thinking, the most critical component of success is how you, as a community, collectively create a vision for your downtown and how you go about making that vision a reality.

We often tell the story of the community group that we met in 1992 (Taylor & Jinks, 1992). This group carried with them the vision they had for their downtown to every meeting they attended. The vision was an artist's watercolor rendition of what they wanted to do with an old, abandoned hotel in their downtown. The picture included a small visual slice of the downtown square surrounding the hotel, showing new streetlights, building facades, and landscaping. When we first met this community group they had no idea how they would make this vision a reality. However, over these past few years we have watched an amazing transformation take place in this community as it turned a vision into bricks and mortar, streetlights, and landscaping. This is but one success story we will share with you as we outline the way you can make your downtown an important part of a total community economic development plan.

DOWNTOWNS: WHERE ARE WE AND HOW DID WE GET HERE?

Trying to maintain downtowns as viable social and economic entities in communities across America has been part of community economic development planning for many years. Downtown development programs probably found their beginnings in the late 1960s, coinciding with the first great threat, what many would see as the bane of downtowns, the advent of the strip shopping center. The federal government took the initial lead in focusing on downtown vitality, a good example being the programs implemented during the heyday of the Model Cities Program with urban renewal and Urban Development Action Grants (UDAGs). More often than not, state and local governments have led the way with innovative initiatives, launching specific programs to meet the needs of individual downtowns. Georgia, Wisconsin, Iowa, Pennsylvania, and New York have been as active as any states, relying most heavily on the Main Street Program as their primary downtown development tool.

Georgia provides a good example of what downtowns mean to a total state economy. With 535 municipalities in Georgia, there is no shortage of downtowns in the state. We are sure that this is the case in your state as well. There are many examples of communities across Georgia, and other states, that have made the downtown areas vital and thriving symbols of success. Improving the central business districts in towns is important for a variety of reasons.

DOWNTOWNS AS A RESOURCE BASE

Downtowns in most communities represent a tremendous investment of time, money, history, and infrastructure. The signature elements of downtowns, the buildings, roads, utilities, and parks in the communities across this country, have been developed over many years. Many downtowns have histories as old as the states in which they are found. The businesses and industries located in these downtowns generate a great deal of employment and tax revenues for their respective states. Their housing and recreational areas provide a wide assortment and diversity of places to live and find entertainment. Moreover, downtowns across this country, a great many with characteristic squares in their downtown areas, are almost always the location of government offices, whether local, state, or federal.

A community's downtown often provides a snapshot of its history and its people and a gauge of its economic vitality. The unique courthouses and city halls found in many communities across this country, places like Blakely, Georgia; Greenfield, Iowa; Winnsboro, South Carolina; and Albany, New York, reflect the commercial and financial influence that these towns now have or once had. The commercial districts in places like Richland, Georgia; Luverne, Alabama; Bryan, Texas; and Hays, Kansas, indicate how vital and thriving these communities once were. More importantly, the attractive tree-lined streets with large old homes and the courthouse squares of many communities, reminiscent of Jimmy Stewart movies, are a continuous reflection of the traditional American value of how important towns are to all of us. Throughout this country, downtowns convey community history, traditions, and evidence of economic vitality to residents and visitors alike.

The buildings in downtowns across this country, from the most unassuming storefront to the most imposing courthouse, represent a sort of iconography of our community economic development history. They reflect the importance that we placed on the uses of these buildings. In many communities across this land, the most impressive downtown buildings—courthouses, libraries, schools, and city halls—house public functions. These are often imposing in size and scale relative to the community that surrounds them, Mount Vernon, Georgia, and Lexington, Georgia, being good examples.

In other communities, usually the larger cities in many states, it is the retail and commercial buildings—stores, offices, and financial institutions—upon which elaborate and unique architectural design was conferred. These buildings have served to symbolize the downtown's role as a center of finance and trade. However, smaller communities often have buildings that were intended to convey statements about the downtown.

One of the most interesting buildings of this type is the Hand Building in Pelham, Georgia. This three story domed building was built in 1916 at a cost of $1 a square foot. It features an open atrium of Italian stained glass and encompasses 97,000 square feet of space. We have seen no other building serving to provide a statement of what its owners dreamed they thought the community would become than this building. It is disappointing to note that the building now stands abandoned but in mint condition. Nevertheless, the building remains as one of the most imposing and aesthetically pleasing buildings we have ever seen.

The development of some Georgia communities into regional trade centers is often symbolized by the vitality of its central business district. No doubt you have seen the same things in your state. Perhaps the best example we can point to, showing how revitalization can occur, is provided by the revival of Atlanta's downtown in the 1970s and 1980s. This, not coincidentally, provided the continued impetus for its growth into a financial and transportation hub of the Southeast. A similar strategy for downtown development is unfolding in Charlotte, North Carolina, and Birmingham, Alabama, as these communities begin to emerge as important economic forces in the Southeast and in the country. Charlotte is using its NationsBank Center and other financial institutions as the focus for downtown development, while Birmingham centers its development around the University Medical Center and its related clinics.

Today, communities in Georgia, such as Tifton, Rome, Commerce, Brunswick, and Valdosta, are strengthening their local and regional economies by attracting new businesses and industries while rebuilding their downtowns. On a smaller scale, other Georgia communities, such as Lumpkin, Newnan, Conyers, and Nashville, are also working to revive their downtowns as part of their overall economic development strategy.

DOWNTOWN DEVELOPMENT THREATS AND OPPORTUNITIES

Why is downtown important to a community's economic development future and why are some in trouble? No doubt, many main streets around the country have changed. Once the vibrant center of civic and commercial life, main streets of many communities began experiencing economic difficulty primarily since the middle of the 20th century. Many succumbed to the restructuring of the agricultural economy, especially in the South, while still others saw increasing out-migration of people, particularly young people, after World War II. More recently, downtowns have faced tough competition. First the competition came from strip shopping centers and later from shopping malls and outlet malls. In addition, other factors, such as changes in consumer lifestyles, commuting patterns, social and economic mobility, and shoppers' expectations of the quality and quantity of goods and services they want available and convenient have had an impact on downtowns.

We see important new trends in competition for small downtowns beyond the recent debates over Wal-Mart's invasion of many rural communities, as evidenced by Home Depot's recent announcement of expansion to these same markets. Several fast food chains, such as Hardee's and McDonald's, have aggressively moved into areas outside small downtowns as well. As vacancy rates in downtowns have increased in many communities across the country, they have triggered a cycle of dis-investment which gradually leads to the loss of economic vital-ity for many communities. In addition, many communities have their greatest investments in infrastructure, such as water, sewer, and transportation, in their downtown areas. This is a significant investment that many communities cannot afford to duplicate or waste.

Another difficult obstacle for downtowns to overcome, and a rather ironic one, has resulted from transportation devel-opments such as the interstate highway system and the emer-gence of the automobile as the predominate form of personal transportation. One negative thing interstate highways initially did to downtowns was take a great many of the casual visitors, the people merely passing through, away from them. The inter-states also accelerated the development of bypass highways that allowed and encouraged traffic to go around the economic hearts of many communities, another blow for downtowns. By-passes and interstates and the automobiles that filled them, fa-cilitated the advent of the strip shopping center and the mall which further exacerbated the demise of downtowns as retail and commercial centers.

Several years ago, a colleague conducted a survey in a large midwestern state (personal correspondence from Jerry Wade, 1988). The survey asked residents of small towns in this par-ticular state such questions as what did they need to "make their community complete," and how would they know when they had "made it" as a town. Overwhelmingly, respondents said a McDonald's and a Wal-Mart would make them a total community. These are two giants who have not typically cho-sen to be downtown anchors.

From a community economic development standpoint should we care? What possible use can we find for downtowns anymore? Haven't changes in retail shopping patterns, where shoppers seemingly give preference to malls and shopping cen-ters, and concerns over crime and parking effectively killed downtown as a viable concept?

Absolutely not! We have recently seen some very innova-tive economic development ideas carried out by communities with the downtown as the focal point. New opportunities, provided by such funding programs as those contained in the Intermodal Surface Transportation Efficiency Act (ISTEA), provide impetus for new initiatives. In addition, we are now witnessing more interest being focused on downtowns by traditional and nontraditional development organizations than ever before in our collective memories. Why? What has brought about this renewed interest in downtowns and what does it mean for your community and your economic development planning?

THE RENEWED FOCUS ON DOWNTOWNS

Several trends have come together to bring about a renewed interest in the future of downtowns. Travel trends, in concert with demographics, now work to the benefit of downtowns. To some degree, interstates have lost their lustre. Increasingly, travelers, especially older travelers, are looking to get off the beaten track, namely the heavily traveled interstates. There is a growing interest in going back and seeing what is on the alternative routes. For example, in Georgia, travelers are returning to preinterstate north/south routes such as U.S. 1, U.S. 441, U.S. 27, and U.S. 411. These highways pass through many small towns and, consequently, their downtowns. Increasingly, demographics, particularly the aging of the population, are providing an impetus for looking for our "community roots" for the comfortable feelings we have about hometowns and downtowns. For the most part, those memories are most likely to be rooted in small town downtowns. How we restore and preserve those vestiges of downtown, i.e., the town square, the courthouse, the department store, the soda fountain, and the park, and, more importantly, how we make them economically viable and attractive, can be a very important part of a total community economic development program.

Another reason renewed focus is being given to downtowns relates to the growing awareness of the large "sunk" investments in downtowns. The largest investor-owned utility in this state, Georgia Power Company, is poised to announce a major initiative in downtown revitalization. Why? Utilities and local governments are coming to the somewhat late realization that they have tremendous economic investments in infrastructure, such as roads, sewers, water, electric power, telecommunications, and buildings that are concentrated in the compact area of downtowns. Given that most new retail and commercial developments are outside of downtowns and given that they require significant new investments in infrastructure by governments and utilities, these entities are getting a new appreciation of the stake they have in the future of downtowns all over the state. This new realization is beginning to happen all over the country.

LESSONS TO BE LEARNED

ICAD recently conducted a study for a quasi-governmental organization that represents city governments in a large southern state. The study was to ascertain the status and situations in downtowns across that state. That downtowns are vitally important was reflected in the 75% return rate for completed surveys. Over 1,500 surveys from the state's elected officials were returned. Almost all cities with populations over 500 responded, a total of 334 communities. Preliminary analysis reveals some important points to consider when building a vision for the future of downtowns.

Three out of four respondents reported that their downtowns were only in fair shape or on the ropes. Of these, 75% reported they had no Mainstreet Program, 54% had no downtown merchant's association, and 50% had no downtown development authority. When asked, "What is the one thing you would do to improve downtown?", overwhelmingly, respondents said they would like a greater variety of stores downtown. This is not exactly a creative response to the problems of downtowns in the 1990s.

GETTING TO A STARTING POINT

Our experiences have shown us that communities and community groups generally pick one of the following areas as starting points for downtown work: general landscaping/ cleanup; downtown organizations; facade improvements; "gateway" projects; "shop local" promotions; the creation of an "anchor"; and/or the development and marketing of the downtown as a tourism attraction. By no stretch of the imagination are these the only projects that can be successful, nor should they be viewed as mutually exclusive categories.

Wrightsville, Georgia, brought together a large segment of the community to do something about the downtown's back alleys. They developed a plan to create a mural of the community's history along these long expanses of wall. School art classes, retirement groups, churches, and social organizations contributed paint and time to create a colorful addition, as well as tourist attraction, to the downtown. In addition, the alleys were landscaped and trash containers were located in common areas behind screens. The community also convinced a local Coca-Cola bottler to repaint the old advertising signs located on many downtown buildings. Other projects snowballed from these including having a nursery donate ferns to downtown merchants to hang from storefront awnings and downtown merchants working several Saturdays to paint the facades of buildings in the downtown area.

Colquitt, Georgia, solicited sponsorship from individuals, families, churches, and civic organizations to place antique street lamps around their downtown square. Initially, the community set a goal of 18 streetlights at $1,000. However, after placing one on the square and having the community see how attractive they were, 28 sponsorships were eventually sold. Each streetlight has a plaque at the base identifying the sponsor. The local office of the Georgia Power Company provided assistance in placing and mounting the lights, as well as agreeing to lifetime maintenance and service. Some other successful downtowns were recently spotlighted in *Parade Magazine*. Clarksville, Missouri, managed to keep its downtown viable with a $2 million, 7 year revitalization project. It decreased the vacancy rate in the downtown area from 86% to 25% and brought in 16 new businesses and 35 new jobs. Dubuque, Iowa, spent 10 years turning five districts into a bustling downtown area. They added 325 new business starts, 968 new jobs, 150 new housing units, a convention center, and waterfront cultural offerings to the community. Franklin, Tennessee, saw its downtown fill with vacant buildings as much of its commerce was siphoned off into nearby Nashville. A decade of work and $2.3 million in public and private funds have turned things around. Sheboygan Falls, Wisconsin, rejuvenated its downtown after volunteers found a way to turn a 19th century wool mill into affordable housing in the heart of downtown. Our point is that downtowns can make it! They can be an important part of your overall community economic development strategy. How can this happen? Let us give you some ideas and suggestions from our work with various communities and community groups.

SOME OBSERVATIONS ON DOWNTOWNS

In summary, we make the following observations given the limitations of extrapolating beyond our experiences with communities. However, we feel these observations have a great deal of application to other communities and downtowns:

- Downtowns don't do well without help and support from the total community, including government, merchants, property owners, and consumers. Our experience has been that many communities see general cleanup/fix up as the most cited need in communities who identify themselves with a downtown that is on the ropes. Local government's leadership is critical in making this happen.
- Downtown development authorities, merchants' associations, and mainstreet programs are critical to the success of downtowns. Communities with viable downtown development au-

thorities and active merchants' associations experience some of the greatest levels of satisfaction and success with their downtowns. We must find ways we can translate the success of the Mainstreet Program into a broader program for more downtowns.

- Government buildings, and government presence in downtowns, are assets. However, it is not always clear what to do with these assets to benefit the downtown. The greatest opportunity for success with downtown revitalization seems to be in cities that are also county seats, primarily because of the concentration of government offices (stable entities), both county and city, in the downtown.
- Planning, especially coordinated planning between all entities interested and/or involved in downtown, has an impact on the success or failure of downtowns.
- Most people see their downtowns as small (reflecting perhaps a bias towards small towns). Small towns, especially those with single main streets and/or no central focus or anchor, suffer the greatest problems of downtown viability.
- People tend to be positive about the future of downtowns.
- People tend not to identify single, dominant assets for their downtowns. They identify a wide variety of things as the most important asset in their downtowns, including government buildings, historic structures, location, physical features, transportation factors, commercial anchors, and small town atmosphere. The point being that there can be a lot of things to build on for the future.
- We need to think creatively about how to use downtowns— to expand our apparent mindset that downtown is only a retail center. We reference most people's response that they would like to see more stores downtown. Given the retailing environment of the 1990s, that is mall and outlet shopping, is a retail center viable for downtowns? If so, it may have to be a "different type" of retail center. Only small downtowns tend to identify more stores as the solution to downtown problems. Given the nature of retailing, this is most likely not a solution to downtown problems. Strategies that look at downtowns not as central business districts, but as central so-

cial districts, portend the greatest opportunity for success. To do this we need to look for ideas that can help us find ways to get more people downtown, e.g., housing or professional services, restaurants, or speciality retailing that can draw people who live and work downtown.

- The more there is a central, identifiable core for a downtown, the more likely that the downtown is viable. We have found, again and again, that communities with their downtowns centered around a square, or some other central focus, are much more likely to view their downtowns as successful.

- Government officials, more often than not, view the level of services they provide to downtowns as excellent in both quality and quantity. In addition, they see the lack of support for downtowns as coming from others, and not from themselves. Governmental services that focus on downtown general maintenance (street sweeping, street repair, building inspection/code enforcement, etc.) correlate most highly with successful/attractive downtowns.

What these observations mean for your downtown you must decide for yourself. However, we see these findings as providing good starting points for discussion of what you might do to make your downtown more viable or to continue to build on your success.

TIPS FOR DOWNTOWN REVITALIZATION

1. Conduct a windshield survey of your downtown area with local leaders and volunteers. What do you see regarding litter, building facades, parking, safety, places to sit and talk, signage, easy access, etc.?
2. Can travellers easily find your downtown area from the bypass, interstate, and major highways?
3. What impression does your downton give to visitors? Does it say: "Come on down and enjoy." "You better not stop because we will give you a ticket." "This is not a safe place." "The people are not friendly."
4. Do you have a downtown merchants' association or group that represents the business interests of the town/community?
5. Is there a cultural heritage, building design, or visual theme for the downtown?
6. Do you have any sort of welcome center or place where visitors' questions can be answered? If so, is it readily identifiable?
7. Are you a Mainstreet Community? Are there other designations in your state for which your downtown can qualify?

CHAPTER 6

Developing Tourism and Recreation Potential

In almost every community economic development discussion we have participated in over the past 10 years, the subjects of tourism and recreation have been raised. Tourism, leisure travel, outdoor learning experiences, and opportunities for recreation are all perceived to bring in money and promote the development of jobs. We get these perceptions from the media: news articles, cable channel features on exotic places for leisure and travel, and movies and special features encouraging us to learn about people and communities in other parts of the world.

This chapter presents information about assessing, developing, and utilizing community assets for tourism and recreational community economic development. We have included examples of how various communities have promoted their unique features to attract visitors to their area. We also include a detailed proposal of how one community, with which we work, is organizing to develop local and natural and wildlife areas as tourism and recreational enterprises. We envision community groups reviewing their unique assets to fit their specific local and area resources.

This chapter reinforces our belief that community economic development is about more than just recruiting industry. We see tourism and recreation as an untapped generator of jobs and income for communities. This chapter also demonstrates that the potential of recreation and tourism as a significant contributor to community economic development is not limited to only communities along coastal areas or in mountain regions.

There are assets everywhere! The challenge for communities is to recognize that they have areas of interest to senior citizens, families, and others who may be, for example, birdwatchers, hunters, hikers, photographers, naturalists, gardeners, history buffs, or antique or paraphernalia collectors, who want a place they can relax, recreate, learn about, and enjoy.

ASSESSING TOURISM AND RECREATION POTENTIAL

Communities have assets! Assets may be found in the form of creative residents or visitors, natural and scenic areas, unique land or vegetation, water resources, vistas, clean air, and manmade features. How a community perceives these assets and organizes the creative potential of local residents are the key elements in promoting tourism.

Tourism

To take advantage of tourism opportunities, expand on your community organizing, act creatively and think of the demographics of people (for example, baby boomers with money and time to travel). One of the best resources we can refer you to on demographics and marketing is *American Demographics*, a very user-friendly magazine that provides excellent information on trends and marketing angles. As you get more skilled in developing tourism possibilities, think about using existing geological and topographic features, unique or rare wildlife and environments, or attractive artist scenery. Keep in mind that there are numerous resources that can help you get started and provide you with information on what to do in terms of funding, grants, etc. An excellent resource is the Rural Information Center at the National Agricultural Library in Beltsville, Maryland. They provide toll-free access to their services at 1–800–633–7701.

What are your community's assets? What does the community have in terms of cultural sites and events, scenic areas, natural areas, climate, agricultural crops, historic sites, buildings and businesses, and unique features in the town or community? What are the contributions of people in the area: did they settle the region, move into the region, develop the region, or change the region in some unique way?

Following is one strategy you can use to assess the unique features of your community. For example, we have identified four topical areas to begin your assessment. These factors include: community history and unique individuals; unique plants and animals; natural structures; and man-made structures/features.

1. Historic Background and Unique Individuals/Groups
   A. What is the historical significance of your community?

   B. Who or what groups settled the area?

   C. Who or what groups moved into the area?

   D. What are the interesting historic and cultural values of local groups?

   E. Were there local residents of state, multi-state, or national prominence (e.g., people who were elected officials, appointed to offices, or made noteworthy discoveries).

   F. What Native Americans lived in your area?

   G. What genealogical resources, family histories, or cemeteries exist, or have been cataloged, for your area.

2. Unique Plants/Animals
   A. What are the unique/unusual plants and animals that are native to your community?

   B. Are there unusual trees or shrubs?

   C. Are there migrations of animals, birds, or insects?

3. Natural Structures
   A. Are there unusual/unique land, sea, river, or stream formations?

   B. Are there interesting weather or climatic features?

C. What about sunsets, sunrises, and the scenic beauty of the area?

D. Does the area have unique geological structures?

4. Man-made Structures/Features

A. Are there unusual man-made structures in the area?

B. Is the community removing man-made structures to revert to a more natural environment?

C. What about downtowns, countrysides, urban, or isolated areas?

D. Are there unique farming practices to prevent erosion and to blend into the natural beauty of the area?

E. What about unique industrial/manufacturing operations which might offer tours?

Recreation

Each community offers a vast array of recreation opportunities. What the community has naturally and what it can create are the building blocks for expanding economic development in the area. Beaches, salt water, fresh water, marshes, streams, lakes, waterfalls, hills, mountains, unique vegetation, animals, clear skies, snow, rainfall, desert—it all depends upon what exists and what senses can be utilized. For example:

1. Observing moon beams a full moon at midnight off of Cumberland Falls near Corbin, Kentucky

2. Canoeing the rivers and marshes of coastal regions in Virginia, North and South Carolina, Georgia, and Florida

3. Snow skiing in New Hampshire or Vermont

4. Fishing and water skiing in the Ozarks

5. Observing the sandhill cranes along the North Platte River in Nebraska

6. Photographing alligators and other wildlife in the Oke-fenokee Swamp in Georgia and Florida

7. Camping along the Allagash River in Maine and listening to the water as it moves on its journey to the sea

8. Watching butterflies hatch at the Sibley Butterfly Center located in Callaway Gardens near Pine Mountain, Georgia

9. White-water rafting on the Snake River in Idaho and Wyoming

10. Hiking in national parks, such as Glacier in Montana and Denali in Alaska

All of these activities take advantage of natural or man made facilities that have attracted visitors to a town or region or park or facility. Hopefully, the number of visitors can be large enough to require services and employ people on a seasonal or annual basis.

COMMUNITY ASSESSMENT EXAMPLE

This is a beginning point for assessing and discussing the community, county, and regional area for tourism and recreation potential. The following is an assessment, listed point by point, of Crawfordville, Georgia's potential.

Location and Demographics

Taliaferro County, Georgia, is a sparsely populated rural county that has a 1,000 acre state park within walking distance of downtown. The climate in the county is mild to moderate for the Piedmont area of Georgia. There are 250 growing days per year with 55 inches of rainfall and 50 days with below freezing temperatures. Major crops grown in the area are soybeans, wheat, and cotton. Major industries include poultry, timber, and lumber products.

The county is divided by I-20 that connects Atlanta with Augusta and has more than 20,000 cars passing by on any given day. There are two rivers, the Ogeechee and the Little, that pass through the county with several large creeks that empty into these rivers. There are numerous wetlands and marshes made possible by beavers damming up small creeks and streams. There are no major lakes or reservoirs in the county.

There are fewer than 2000 residents in the county with average per capita income of $14,464, which is below the state average of $18,549. There are few young people raising families in the county. Population characteristics indicate that about one-fifth (19.2%) of the population are older adults over 65 and a slightly higher percentage (23.4%) are youth 5–19 years of age, while another one-fifth of the population (19.3%) are younger adults of 20–34 years of age. The percentage of adults over age 25 who have completed high school or higher is 22%.

Downtown Crawfordville

Downtown Crawfordville has been the scene for eight major motion pictures and several made for television movies. Also, more than 20 television productions have used scenes from the downtown or rural countryside in the county. Community leaders and business owners have decided to keep the downtown in the 1940—1950 period and maintain facades, sidewalks, streets, building designs, and remodeling to reflect this era. A University of Georgia class of historic preservation students recently completed an inventory of the houses and buildings in the town according to time period, construction, and historic significance.

Unique Features

There are three historic churches in the county, two springs which have been or currently are being promoted for bottled water, and a unique walk-through Christmas lighting display, Christmas in Dixie, that draws almost 100,000 visitors to the county during the Christmas and New Year holiday season. There is a museum featuring Alexander H. Stephens, who was vice president of the Confederate States during the Civil War; plantation life in middle Georgia; and the historic culture of the 1800s. Several farms have homes that were on stage coach routes through the state in the late 1700s and early 1800s. Some of the homes have been in continuous use as dwellings, bed and breakfast inns, and productive farms since their construction.

Community Organizations

Several different groups, such as the Historic Society, Downtown Merchants' Association, Park Preservation and Development, Rural Development, and local church associations, are working toward the development of the downtown and county. However, they do not seem to be working together except for a few community members who are in several of these different groups or associations.

Local residents are indeed proud and concerned about the potential for development in their community and county. They are also divided in their points of view about the types of development, the impact of development on rural life styles, and the implications of these changes on race relations.

Summary

An overall assessment of Crawfordville, Georgia, is that it is a "sleeping giant" about to be awakened by tourists from I-20 looking for historic sites and cultural features. Tourists will be looking for recreation sites and services such as, the Alexander H. Stephens State Park and Museum; a place to eat, such as Ms. Bonners Cafe; and a place to lodge—a bed and breakfast inn is being considered near downtown within walking distance of the Stephens Museum.

Visitors will want to visit downtown shops and other sites such as the proposed television and movie museum, while in Crawfordville. During the holiday season visitors will be able to participate in a special lighted walking tour of "Christmas in Dixie." It is proposed that during the spring, summer, and fall there will be camping, fishing, biking, boating, swimming, and triathlons held at the Alexander H. Stephens Park. The single missing ingredient is a chamber of commerce or development authority or organization with enough financial support to promote this area to the general public that passes by it each day on the interstate.

DEVELOPING TOURISM AND RECREATION POTENTIAL

To develop tourism and recreation potential, community leaders and volunteers need to think about what motivates people to select tourism and recreation activities. For example, motivating factors can include opportunities for: relaxation, learning, activity, socializing, competing, escaping, or creating. The following motivations should provide you with ideas on how to develop local tourism and recreation potential.

1. Relaxation — Focus on activities or sites that facilitate relaxation. For example, hiking and biking trails, nature walks, and bird watching can provide an atmosphere for relaxation.

2. Learning — Promote activities that facilitate learning. For example, people want to learn about historic or cultural features of an area.

3. Activity — Provide around opportunities to do something for the community or for personal improvement. For example, community leaders and volunteers could sponsor an environmental education and cleanup activity in a wetlands area.

4. Socializing — Offer opportunities to meet interesting local residents. For example, introduce tourists to potters, weavers, blacksmiths, artists, photographers, authors, and musicians in the community.

5. Competing — Challenge visitors to test their skills against nature. For example, rafting, canoeing, climbing, orienteering, and running.

6. Escaping — Invite tourists to get away from it all. For example, excursions to remote areas, farm vacations, and dude ranches provide tourists with a chance to get away from everyday monotony and stress.

7. Creating — Offer visitors the opportunity to create personal contributions to a process or product. For example, participants might help rehabilitate dilapidated housing, refurbish parks, reseed forest lands, or catalog historic sites.

Additional Strategies for Developing Tourism/Recreation

Another strategy for developing tourism and recreation in an area is to look at the travel (or migration) patterns of people. Where and how do people travel? What highways and travel patterns do they use? Do they use interstates, major highways, or secondary roads? What are their destinations and how many days do they spend getting to their destinations? What are their modes of travel—air planes, automobiles, boats, trains, bicycles, etc? State and regional (multi-state) demographics can help identify potential travel patterns as well as specify motivational trends for recreation and tourism.

A suggested plan for developing your community's tourism and recreation potential could begin with some of the following ideas:

1. Conduct a community assets inventory.

2. Identify people willing to work on this activity.

3. Identify local, state, and regional population characteristics.

4. Determine what people want (re: motivation for travel, recreation, and tourism).

5. Look for matches between community assets and what motivates people to travel.

6. Look for multiple options to develop; recreation and retirement are two areas that successful communities promote.

7. "Toot your own horn" about community assets in magazines, newspapers, cable television, and on-line computer networks—if you don't do it nobody else will.

UTILIZING TOURISM FOR COMMUNITY ECONOMIC DEVELOPMENT

Baker City, Oregon (Cole, 1994), developed a tourism strategy that has turned around their economic development picture. In a recent *Small Town* magazine article, Brian Cole described the community economic development activities of a small town in the northeast corner of Oregon. Baker City is located near I-84 and the Oregon Trail. Community leaders and residents decided to capitalize on their location and to develop a strategy to get I-84 travellers to stop in their town.

In brief, Baker City residents designed a plan that included building an interpretative center to highlight the Oregon Trail. In the first 9 months over 300,000 visitors stopped at the center. Expanding their economic development plan, the community added facilities to get visitors to stay overnight in Baker City. As their success continued to draw visitors, community leaders looked for other attractions to promote for tourism. Access to Hells Canyon on the Snake River was another potential for development. More people came to Baker City, and more attractions were promoted including the Brownlee Reservoir, historic sites, an expanded historic district downtown, and the renovation of a historic downtown hotel. These are only a few of the projects undertaken by Baker City with interest and support from the state and various federal government agencies including the U.S. Forest Service, the National Historic Trust, the National Main Street Center, and various state and regional tourism associations.

What did Baker City do to enhance their community? They expressed their concern for community economic development, designed a plan for improvements, and identified a focus, which was their proximity to the Oregon Trail. From preliminary studies they sought local and state support to build an interpretative center. They market their center to the public driving up and down I-84. They kept expanding their plan and connecting their community to other tourist attractions in their county and region. They were able to build partnerships with local, state, and federal agencies to seek funding and support for their community vision.

Festivals as Tourist Attractions

Cooperative extension professionals in Illinois have organized materials for developing and hosting festivals in communities. One of their successful case studies is a community that has sponsored a crafts and agricultural related festival for over 20 years that brings over $2 million into the county on an annual basis.

What could your community do with an activity that generated $2 million annually to promote crafts and agricultural products in the county and surrounding areas? Economists estimate that this money is subject to a multiplier effect of seven times, so the impact for the area is closer to $14 million on an annual basis.

Who benefits from these festivals? People who attend the festival when they have fun, see new craft ideas, purchase gifts for family or friends, and enjoy a relaxing time with friends and family; craftspeople who design and create items for display or sale have invested their time, money, and creativity in making the crafts and thinking about how they will display their skills; organizers of the festival who get satisfaction from putting on a successful event where attendance increases each year and the problems they have to work out with local residents and merchants are translated into income and goodwill for the community; local merchants, who may be inconvenienced for a few days with traffic and noise, also may find people interested in their products and services; merchants who may be the shopping source for craftspeople who do their shopping locally; and suppliers of local merchants who benefit from filling orders and providing services to accommodate getting ready for and hosting the festival.

Leisure and Learning Tours

The idea of elderhostels and youth hostels has spread throughout the world. Individuals can locate hundreds of cities, towns, villages, and communities that offer several days accommodations and the opportunity to learn about the geography, geology, flora, fauna, historic features, interesting people, and a host of other topics. The purpose of the "hostel" idea is to offer an inexpensive yet practical learning experience in an enjoyable atmosphere for participants.

Elderhostels have been so well accepted and patronized that some communities are offering "institutes" or seminars or community Chautauquas (i.e., 18th-century style town hall meetings) for participants to live and learn about small towns and rural areas. Community institutes are another way of trying to attract tourists to their area to enjoy, relax, learn, and possibly come back to live or retire in the community. Some former elderhostel and institute participants have liked some communities so much that they invest in businesses, bed and breakfast inns, and retirement homes in the area.

Local Cultural History

Colquitt, Georgia

One community in southwest Georgia developed a play about the local culture, family interactions, business transactions, and historical events of the area. They call this play *Swamp Gravy* (Jones, 1994). A brochure about *Swamp Gravy* says:

> *Swamp Gravy* gleans the comedy and the tragedy of daily life from family stories, tall tales and folk tales from southwest Georgia. It celebrates the culture that is uniquely rural Georgia.

Swamp Gravy was designed as a community play with multiple characters played by a cross section of the residents in the small town of Colquitt located in Miller County, Georgia. "Pretty near everybody in Colquitt is on stage to welcome you and tell about the amazing adventures of this peanut butter and mayhaw jelly town."

Arlington, Vermont

In Arlington, Vermont, the Norman Rockwell Museum provides an extensive collection of Norman Rockwell's paintings, lithographs, and magazine covers. Rockwell made Arlington his home early in his career. Many of the local citizens posed for Rockwell's artwork and serve as docents in the museum.

Nebraska City, Nebraska

In Nebraska City, Nebraska, the Arbor Foundation has captured the spirit of a community that saw the need to plant trees as a way of everyday life by establishing a National Arbor Day. As the Arbor Day idea has caught on and expanded over the years, the Foundation saw the need for building a conference center for participants and tourists to learn about conservation while enjoying a relaxing and restful meeting space. Heating of the conference center is done by burning wood products grown on the Arbor Foundation property.

Atlanta, Georgia

The Apex Museum located on Auburn Avenue in the historic African-American community of Atlanta promotes the

cultural heritage of blacks who were brought to this country
as slaves and have risen to positions of leadership and prominence in this developing nation. The Apex is the "gateway" to
the historic Auburn Avenue district in downtown Atlanta. Over
100,000 visitors, scholars, historians, and tourists come to the
Apex Museum on an annual basis. This number is expected to
multiply 10 times during and after the 1996 Olympics. Currently the museum serves as one of the few collections of artifacts and displays of African-American culture in the United
States. Thousands of school children visit the museum during
Black History Month which is celebrated in February of each
year.

Cody, Wyoming

The Wild Bill Cody Museum located in the small town of
Cody, Wyoming, is an attraction for visitors and tourists to the
Western states. For the hiker, biker, fisherman, and visitor to
Yellowstone National Park, the Wild Bill Cody Museum is an
opportunity to pause and reflect on the development of the Old
West. Over a million visitors pass through the Cody Museum
on an annual basis providing an economic benefit of $5 million
for food, lodging, transportation, and related products and
services.

PROMOTION OF NATURAL AND WILDLIFE
AREAS AND RESOURCES: A PROPOSAL FOR
DISCUSSION AND DEVELOPMENT

The following is a suggested outline for promoting wildlife areas and natural resources of the community. Items are
presented in an outline format for a small group or subcommittee to complete and present to a local board or potential funding source. Parts of this outline will need to be changed or expanded to reflect the unique characteristics of your community.

Inventory of Natural and Wildlife Areas

You will need to expand this inventory to reflect the diversity of your region. These are some of the key resources that you may have in your community, or area, that are potential attractors for tourists and recreation enthusiasts.

1. Water (lakes, rivers, streams)

2. Forests (state parks, forests, and private holdings)

3. Air (clean air)

4. Soil (rich sandy soils for row crop production)

5. Natural areas (parks, Indian mounds, lakes, rivers, streams, and swamps)

6. Wildlife (deer, turkey, quail, dove, song birds, birds of prey, etc.)

7. Fisheries (bass, bream, trout, catfish, etc.)

The county and surrounding communities may have an abundance of opportunities, both public and private, for outdoor sports, recreation, and relaxation. Your community group will also need to be aware of public and private ownership factors as they relate to these resources. These factors may include such things as: access to land for hunting, fishing, photography, or camping; hunting and fishing rights; land leases and pricing for recreation or hunting and fishing. All of these factors should be negotiated before any of these activities are encouraged or marketed to tourists or recreation enthusiasts.

Specific Examples for Promoting Natural Areas and Wildlife

1. Quail hunting on both public and private lands may currently be promoted on a few of the established farms in surrounding counties. There may be other private land-

owners who would either lease their land to established quail hunting preserves or form a consortium of property owners for someone to manage and promote for quail hunting.

2. Turkey hunting is one of the fastest growing sports in the United States. A turkey habitat consists of hardwood bottomlands with interspersed fields and openings for birds in search of food and companionship. A consortium of private landowners could be encouraged to lease their properties or to form a federation of holdings that are managed for turkey. Turkey and deer management can be coordinated with quail management to give the individual or consortium landowner a higher return on his or her investment.

3. Deer hunting is a traditional event that is enjoyed throughout the United States. Deer management is moving toward "trophy buck" production by attempting to reduce the herd through harvesting does and mature bucks. Bucks with a 16 inch and larger antler spread are being harvested leaving younger, and sometimes better formed, antlered animals to mature. As mentioned above, deer, quail, and turkey can be managed on the same property with some integrating of land use and timber management techniques.

4. Wild or feral hogs may also be included in the hunting management techniques for deer and turkey.

5. Fishing for bass, bream, and catfish are other sporting traditions that offer opportunities for surrounding counties. Lodges at lakes are an example of promoting the fishery resources both in and outside the region. Spring, fall, and winter (summer may be too hot—check with local fisheries) are beautiful times of the year to fish plantation farm ponds, natural streams, lakes, and rivers in the region.

6. Float fishing expeditions on rivers, creeks, or in lakes offer recreation opportunities for individuals looking for comfortable weather and local hospitality.

7. One of the untapped resources of the region is photography. Individuals interested in unique flowers, plants of the region, and birds of prey (e.g., hawks and owls) will find the region bountiful and a challenge for their photographic skills.

8. Other natural and wildlife resources include preservation and study of Indian artifacts and culture native to the region. Indian mounds and other Native American sites in the region offer an opportunity to study and learn about native cultures.

9. There are numerous swamps, marshes, and wetlands found in the region that offer the explorer, naturalist, photographer, hunter, and fisherman a worthy challenge to visit, observe, and learn about the environment.

10. Bird watching is an activity for the entire family. Plantation owners, farmers, and city dwellers in the region can promote songbirds by building birdhouses, planting food plots, slightly modifying crop harvesting techniques, and generally improving the habitat for song birds.

These 10 items are examples of natural and wildlife habitat areas that communities can promote for community economic development purposes. You may have other ideas for natural and wildlife habitat areas that are unique to your area that can be identified and added to the above list.

Support Facilities

Additional spin-off businesses that can benefit local economic development can come from support facilities that provide services and products to visitors of your local natural and wildlife habitat areas. Some examples of ideas related to support facilities for natural and wildlife habitat improvements include shooting ranges such as rifle, pistol, sporting clays, and archery. For promoting the continued development of the region for tourism and recreation, it is important that your development efforts be cognizant of the need for corollary businesses and services that support your efforts in marketing and promoting your natural and wildlife habitat areas.

1. There may be a need for a bookstore to sell publications related to bird watching, Native American culture, fishing, hunting, hiking, and water sports.

2. Photographic supplies and 24-hour developing services will be needed for visitors to take advantage of the multiple photo opportunities in the county and region.

3. Instruction and "schools" for beginners, as well as experts, in fly-fishing techniques, preparing native foods and dishes, photography, plant identification, Native American folklore, canoeing, rafting, water sports, swamp vegetation and wildlife, ecological systems, and changes in the region.

4. Artists can capture, for promotion and sale in local galleries, sunsets, sunrises, waterfowl, wildlife, and scenic beauty on paper and canvas for visitors to the region. Postcards and greeting cards displaying historic sites, plants, animals, and unique features of the county and region could be displayed to remind the visitor, as well as resident, of the natural beauty in the region.

The overall desired outcome from recognizing, promoting, and improving natural and wildlife habitat areas is to make the region a multipurpose and multiuse area that takes advantage of climate, existing land use practices, water, wildlife, and natural areas.

MARKETING AND PROMOTION OF THE COUNTY AND REGION

Outdoor recreation can be promoted to all ages, genders, and economic levels. Counties and the region offer the individual or family rugged, primitive camping and exploring, or the more relaxed and modern bird watching and photography.

Your region can be an outdoor person's delight. It can offer multiple opportunities for rest, relaxation, and learning in a relaxed environment.

Some examples of seasonal resources and activities are:

- Fall: quail hunting, photography, fishing, deer hunting
- Winter: quail hunting, photography, fishing, deer hunting
- Spring: turkey hunting, photography, fishing, bird watching
- Summer: fishing, photography, bird watching, flowers of the region

To help market your area in the best possible light engage local residents in cleanup and preservation activities and solicit help from visitors to volunteer several days or weekends to assist in these activities. These improvements are more than just the removal of litter along the road, they can also include such things as recycling (e.g., paper, glass, aluminum), fixing up substandard housing and buildings, and cleaning up water systems (e.g., lakes, rivers, streams, and swamps).

Marketing Your Community Environment

Market the attitude of community environment for rest, relaxation, and learning. Make the county and the region accessible by telecommunications (e.g., Internet, national and international communication webs, etc.), roads (e.g., state highways and especially interstates), and by coordinating publicity (e.g., with adjoining counties in the region, state agencies, and statewide economic developers). Another way of marketing the community environment concept is to advertise in publications related to natural areas, photography, water sports, artists, fishing, bird watching, hunting, camping, restoration, and historic preservation. Offer scholarships ($500-$1,000) for members and student members of the above-mentioned professional societies to paint a sunset/sunrise, write a short story, or take photographs. With each scholarship, put in the requirement for publication or display at professional societies to generate interest outside the region and around the world. Invite representatives of the above-mentioned organizations, as well as citizen organizations, (e.g., Sierra Club, National Wildlife Federation, etc.) to attend meetings, classes, and events about preserving and managing wildlife and water sports areas.

Coordination

Somebody, or some agency, must be responsible for coordinating and reporting on the multiple activities of residents, visitors, and agencies serving the county and region. This coordinator could be a full or part-time staff member of a local civic organization, the local chamber of commerce, or some other agency to be designated.

All organizations and agencies in the community and region could be involved in promoting the community environment. For example, the local hotel could assist. The hotel staff could work with the coordinator to offer hospitality, lodging, and dining in the community. Tour guides would offer walking tours, driving tours, outdoor sports, and related packages for the city, county, and region. The hotel reservations staff would be the booking agents for visitors, whether they come to stay one or several days. Local restaurants, antique shops, businesses, and just about anyone in the "meeting the public" industry would function as a booking agent for a visitor.

To take advantage of the trend toward weekend getaway vacations, communities, through a booking agent, could call a coordinator and arrange for a tour or visit to a plantation or for participation in a weekend restoration activity or project. Restoration activities may include monitoring pollution levels in lakes and rivers, collecting recyclables along streams, or repair work in parks and recreation areas.

Planning for Tourism and Recreation Ventures

Inventory landowners in your area who are interested and willing to adopt new management practices and learn new up-to-date environmental and wildlife management techniques. Determine who is interested and who will participate in the planning or implementation of the community environment. Next, check out the hospitality industry such as, lodging, restaurants, churches, businesses, and other recreation interests, such as golf courses and tennis facilities, to see if they will provide a "booking agent" type of participation and support. Then develop and price the packages. For example, a local lodge at a state park could offer a Double Birdies Package, such as, golf and quail hunting, on selected weekends during the fall and winter months.

There may be opportunities for retreats and team building outings for corporate and professional groups, to include golf, fishing, rope challenge courses, and other outdoor activities. Develop packages that emphasize: the family, such as, camping, hunting and fishing; couples, who might participate in golf, fishing, or hunting; and individuals who might have special interests, such as, birdwatching, photography, or nature walks.

Build into the package lodging at local hotels, motels, or bed and breakfast inns, with one or more meals being provided by local restaurants or from agencies sponsoring special events, such as, barbeque suppers at local churches or civic clubs.

SUMMARY

Community groups need to think about the possibilities and potentials of recreation and tourism sites that are within, or nearby, their communities. We emphasize that all too often these recreation and tourism possibilities are overlooked and untapped. Too many economic development professionals are still looking for salvation on the backs of trucks and trains.

We like to tell the story of the Pacific Islanders, who during World War II, became overly dependent on the U.S. Air Force for their daily living. Until the war, these people had been totally self-sufficient. They grew what they needed and fished for what they ate. When the war came they were no longer able to be self-reliant and grew dependent on supplies which were

flown in by allied planes using their island airstrip. These islanders became part of what is known as *cargo cults*. They became overly dependent on the cargo from the planes and when
the war ended they became incapable of returning to their old
ways of life.

We see many communities which are modern day cargo
cults. They wait for economic development to come to them on
the backs of trucks, trains, and consultants. They only see economic development as coming from outside the community.
Our intention with this chapter has been to demonstrate how
communities can generate their own economic development opportunities if they will take the time to study, inventory, and
plan. We have seen jobs and income result from communities
assessing, developing, and utilizing their assets for tourism and
recreation development.

TIPS FOR RECRUITING RETIREES TO THE COMMUNITY

1. Provide information about housing; purchase, rental, time/cost share, listings, phone contacts, etc.
2. Develop lists of services available to retirees moving into your community.
3. Develop brochures and visuals for retirees about services, events, and facilities.
4. Build in procedures for inviting retirees to take part in existing organizations, associations and groups to bring them into the community and to tap into their expertise.
5. Promote recreational, cultural, historic, and learning facilities (e.g., golf courses, tennis facilities, pools, jogging/walking tracks, plays, museums, libraries, and evening and weekend schools) to new members of the community.
6. Introduce retirees and others moving into the community, to the available health care (doctors, hospitals, clinics, home health care, etc.) and protection (animal control, fire, and police) services.
7. Offer opportunities for involving retirees to volunteer for community events, plays, festivals, and recreational events.
8. Provide information about estate planning and everyday financial services.
9. Assign responsibilities for information and personal contacts to invite new people into the social, economic, cultural, religious, and recreational fabric of your village, town, community, or county.

TIPS FOR TOURISM, RECREATION, HISTORIC PRESER-VATION, AND CULTURAL EVENTS

Communities that develop and promote recreation, historic preservation and cultural events can enhance local participation but they also have the potential for expanding their tourism base as a direct result. For this reason, we include all of these concepts under one heading.

1. Inventory the unique features such as recreation, historic preservation, and cultural events in your county, adjoining counties, and the region.
2. Inventory the tourism sites if they are not included in the unique features list in your county, adjoining counties, and the region.
3. List and promote the support facilities such as hotels, motels, bed and breakfast inns, restaurants, public restrooms, parking, handicapped access, laundries, camping areas, and outdoor supply stores, their hours and prices.
4. Look for gaps in your inventories. Does the community or region have enough support facilities? Is there a unique feature or tourism site in every quadrant of your county, adjoining counties, or the region? What is the access and transportation support for unique features and tourism?
5. Regarding fees or taxes: should the community offer these unique features free to draw in visitors or should each site charge a fee?
6. Develop a marketing and promotion strategy to recruit different groups to individual unique features. For example, cross-country bikers would be interested in bike trails, public restrooms, camping facilities, and scenic sites. Canoers, boaters, and rafters would be interested in streams, rivers and lakes, camping, food services, and outdoor supplies. People interested in antiques and restored homes would be interested in a walking tour with signs and brochures, food services, building supplies, craftspeople who did the restora-

tions, and design services. Different groups may be targeted based upon the unique feature or tourist attraction.

7. Promote and provide information, education, and training for owners, operators, and service personnel at all of the sites in the community. These are the people who relate to the public and they provide a lasting impression on visitors. For example, we have all heard the comment, "Those are the nicest people over in Funville. They seemed to enjoy talking to us and providing information on where we could go and what we could do."

CHAPTER 7

Action Planning in the Community: Applications to Industrial Recruitment and Business Retention and Expansion

Your community is only one of many communities actively competing in the economic development arena of traditional industrial/business attraction and retention. The important players in this competition, the industrial prospects and other business firms who are looking for locations for new start-ups or the expansion of existing businesses, compare the qualities of your community with those of other communities to select the location that best meets *their* overall requirements. Do not forget that the requirements of some industries and businesses for a profitable site are not necessarily improved by your efforts at making your community better. However, the more informed you are about what particular businesses and industries are looking for in a site the better you can become at your decision making relative to what you want your community economic development action planning to accomplish. The action learning/planning model we described in Chapter 2 is particularly relevant to your efforts at competing in the arena of traditional business/industry attraction and retention.

Like competitors in any field, each community has special qualities that differentiate it from the other communities who are competing for the limited number of industrial/business prospects in today's global economy. Like any competing team, your community will have some features that are strong and some that are weak. This chapter is about how you can use the action planning process to enhance your community's positive qualities and improve your community's ugly babies. To that end, the way you make your progression from data to information to knowledge will go a long way in determining your success in this competition.

The first step in putting together a sound community economic development action plan is a careful and honest self-analysis of what your community has to offer and what you want your community to be (Brooks, 1991, March). There are several questions you may want to have your community group think about. For example, ask what are your community's strengths and weaknesses? What are your community's needs relative to industrial and business development? You also need to ask what your community's strengths and weaknesses are from the perspective of the kinds of industry and business firms in which you are interested. You will find a variety of experts who can provide you with any number of classification methods which have been devised to define the factors important in the selection of a site for a new facility. It is important to realize that the various methods require a caveat derived from the axiom that you should always make sure you are comparing apples with apples. For example, you would need different kinds of information, community infrastructure, and different classification methods for locating a steel mill versus a poultry processor. Further, this could be illustrated by communities who may fail to locate the steel mill, yet take the same information and pursue a poultry processor.

The same is true of the variety of classification methods available to you. Some are tailored to the needs of manufacturing facilities; others are structured with research and development operations or distribution centers in mind. Many communities find that comprehensive economic development planning is usually best when it is not limited to a single type of facility. We encourage communities early on to conduct a general community economic development assessment before more specific targeting plans are incorporated into a full-fledged action planning.

One starting point is having your group outline those factors that you all think are important to a firm's decision-making process in choosing a location. Obviously, there are certain factors that will influence a location decision. In our experience, these have been some of the factors that community groups and firms have seen as important in recruiting/siting business and/or industry:

- The real estate maxim of location, location, location
- Resources
- Labor force
- Sites
- Capital
- Incentives
- Taxes and fees
- Quality of life

These factors differ in their impact on community quality and on economic development investment decisions by firms. Our feeling is that you, and others in the community, know a lot about these factors as they relate to your community. Put your resource of knowledge to work to evaluate how your community stacks up relative to these factors.

Location factors, such as proximity to markets, must be considered first when selecting a site for a manufacturing production facility, a distribution center, or a business/professional service office. On the other hand, location is not as important when selecting a site for an administrative office or a back-office/catalog order center, especially given the potential for overcoming market problems with telecommunications technologies. National firms like L. L. Bean and Cabelas have proven that with today's technology you don't need to be right next door to your market. Telecommunications make your product easily accessible to worldwide markets.

One effective technique we have used with community economic development groups is the community assessment matrix (Figure 7.1). Community groups are encouraged to think of those factors that pull businesses, people, and industries to the community and those factors that push businesses, people, and industries away. The factors are sorted into quality of life and economic categories. It is important to note, that individuals, groups, or communities evaluate and select from among economic and quality of life factors based upon their assessment of the overall quality of the factor and its affordability. In Figure 7.1, quality and affordability are what we call the *bridge concepts* between the economic considerations and the quality of life factors. The matrix can be used for general assessments or for more targeted strategies and more specific kinds of targeting exercises.

Suppose a warehousing/distribution facility for a major supermarket chain was looking for a site in your area. It would be a very useful exercise to sit down with your community economic development planning team and fill in the matrix. What would be the economic factors, such as labor force, wage levels, infrastructure, taxes, and other businesses that you think could serve to attract such a facility to your community? What would be the economic factors that would cause the supermarket chain not to give your community consideration as a site? At the same time, what are those quality of life factors, such as housing, health care, education facilities/service, crime, recreation, general community services, and support networks that would make you a viable site for such a facility? Again, what quality of life factors would work to your detriment for such a facility? Keep in mind that your efforts will be much better spent if you have done significant homework beforehand on what such a facility is looking for in a site. Your state industrial development offices and site selection magazines such as *Area Development; Plants, Sites, and Parks*; and, *Site Location Magazine* would be useful resources.

We think it is important to remind communities that in many cases one factor, profitability, drives the location decision process for firms. Profitability for a particular site or community is determined by a firm analyzing the mix (costs) of the factors we have listed for your community, relative to other sites or communities that fit their needs. Keep in mind that how you evaluate these factors from the perspective of your community will not always correlate with how particular types of firms may evaluate these same factors for their purposes. For example, if you work hard to improve your community's infra-

PUSHES

PULLS

	PUSHES	**PULLS**
ECONOMIC	• What are the economic factors that push people, business, or industry away from your community? • Why do these factors push people, business, or industry away?	• What are the factors that pull people, business, or industry into your community? • Why do these factors pull people, business, or industry into your community?
QUALITY OF LIFE	• What are the quality of life factors that push people, business, or industry away from your community? • Why do these factors push people, business, or industry away?	• What are the quality of life factors that pull people, business, or industry into your community? • Why do these factors pull people, business, or industry into your community?

• **ECONOMIC** ⟵ Quality and Affordability are two evaluative criteria for discussing these questions. ⟶ • **QUALITY OF LIFE**

What is the QUALITY of a factor and/or is it AFFORDABLE to the community or to people, business, or industry?

Jobs/Labor
Income
Infrastructure
Sewer, water, transportation
Taxes
Retail/Commercial

Housing
Health Care
Education
Crime
Recreation
Community

Figure 7.1 Community assessment matrix

structure, including not just water, sewer, solid waste, transportation, and utilities, but also government, education, housing, and other quality of life factors as well, you may be making your community a more costly site for some types of firms. Choosing whether to be a quality community or a low-cost site is not always a mutually exclusive process, nor do they necessarily coincide. However, that is something you as a community have to decide for yourself.

LOCATION, LOCATION, LOCATION

As we have pointed out earlier, industries and businesses, keeping an eye on the bottom line, want to sell and deliver their product or service to customers and clients. We remind communities that profitability is important for them as well, but that profitability from the perspective of the community is more expansive in that it includes not only economic costs but social and political ones as well. Facilities that are engaged in the marketing, production, distribution, and servicing of goods should have quick and cost-competitive access to these customers and clients. Access in some cases does depend on location as it relates to proximity and the quality and cost of available transportation and/or communications services in your community or immediate area.

It is cheaper and easier to sell, deliver, and service a product if the facility is located in the same community or nearby. So, one consideration in site selection is the size of the local and regional market, especially the size of the market that is not currently served locally or regionally or that is undeserved by competitors. Nearness to output/product markets is not necessarily important because of modern telecommunications and transportation, but this depends on the type of product. Rural communities may have a cost advantage because they are far from population centers. Communities near resources should target economic sectors for which location to those resources is important. Rural communities and, more importantly, communities not near important resources should target economic sectors for which closeness to resources and/or markets is not as important.

The time involved in getting a product or service to its market(s) and the cost of delivering a product or service, not distance, are the important factors for business and industry. The size of the geographic area within which a community can offer competitive access to markets for manufactured goods is determined by its access to transportation services for the movement of goods.

Manufactured goods can be moved from the production facility to the customer via truck, rail, water, or aircargo service. Your community's economic development planning should document your access to and the relative cost of each of these modes of transportation. Some communities have a competitive advantage because they are situated on major rail-freight routes. Others have a competitive advantage because they are located on major interstate highways. Still others benefit from their closeness to an airport that offers extensive aircargo services. For communities on the coast or along a major river, port facilities may provide the competitive edge.

Business and professional services can be exported outside your immediate regional market. Engineers and architects, for example, often serve national and even international markets. The same is true of lawyers, accountants, and consultants. This type of service is becoming known as the creation of "lone eagles," that is, services for which telecommunications can provide advantages regardless of location. The capacity of these lone eagle businesses to serve such export markets is determined by the quality of the air passenger and telecommunications services available in or near the community.

Administrative headquarters and association offices do not serve markets in the traditional sense. The headquarters should, however, have access to other company facilities. Some companies accomplish this by locating their headquarters near their production and distribution centers. Larger companies with facilities spread throughout the country or the world cannot solve their location requirements so simply. Like professional and trade associations whose members are scattered throughout the country, they should have access to their markets by means of air passenger transportation and telecommunications services.

Accordingly, your community economic development action planning should document your nearness to a commercial airport, the number of airlines that serve the area, the number of flights offered, the number of destinations served directly, and the comparative cost of air passenger transportation services in the area.

Technological innovations in telecommunications and in information processing have created new ways in which products and services can be sold and in which some types of client services can be delivered. Telemarketing is a major industry and is expected to grow in the coming years. Today, financial services are delivered electronically. Reservations services (e.g., lodging, car rental, conference registration, airline) and information retrieval services are offered by means of telecommunications systems linked to computers. The people that provide these services can be located almost anywhere.

Administrative offices conduct much of their business with employees in other locations through telecommuting. Communications services offer an alternative to air transportation for some business and professional services and many administrative operations. Citicorp's choice of a location in South Dakota, for their credit card processing offices, was dictated not by traditional factors, such as proximity to markets and access to transportation, but by telecommunications capabilities. Telecommunications makes many otherwise uncompetitive communities highly competitive. Again, some communities have specifically marketed their rural location to lone eagle types. Your community's economic development planning should contain information on the character and comparative cost of communications services available locally, types of services offered, capacity and reliability of systems, and investments in new hardware (such as digital switches and fiber optic cables) which are planned or existing.

RESOURCES

Facilities should have access to the markets they serve. In addition, facilities should have access to the resources used in the course of their operations. The resources consumed are determined by the operations performed in a facility. In your community economic development planning, you should evaluate the availability of each type of resource your community has. There are five such community resource types:

1. Energy

2. Water

3. Raw materials

4. Value-added manufactured goods

5. Business and professional services

Energy Reliability and Cost

All facilities consume energy, whether electricity or natural gas. Accordingly, access to adequate supplies of dependable and affordable electrical and natural gas services is a factor in any location decision. Cost is obviously of greater importance in choosing a site for a production facility that uses large quantities of electricity such as the Southwire Company in Carrollton, Georgia, or Georgia Pacific located in Cedar Springs, Georgia, than for an administrative or marketing office/facility.

For some types of facilities, reliability is even more important than cost. Information processing centers with large numbers of computers should have reliable and stable electrical energy to avoid the loss of data bases or the disruption of services usually associated with what has become known as "brown outs." The same is true for an administrative office operation. Many types of manufacturing operations, such as frozen food or plastics manufacturers, would sustain heavy losses from energy surges or temporary failures. Your community economic development action planning should document local sources of electrical and natural gas services, generating capacities, performance characteristics, and pricing structures together with trend data on rate increases. Local utilities can provide this information to you.

Water

Industry and business firms are major water consumers, whether their need for water is in processing and/or manufacturing or for fire protection services. They need to be concerned with whether the community has sufficient water resources and treatment facilities to meet requirements and support reasonable population growth in the future. Manufacturing operations, such as food processors, chemical manufacturers, or electronic manufacturers need large water supplies. To determine whether your community can meet the needs of this type of industry and to document your ability to satisfy the normal requirements of other types of facilities, your action planning should describe the sources of water for local consumption, the capacity of existing and planned water treatment systems in the area, and the local cost of water and sewerage.

Raw Materials

Some manufacturing operations are heavy users of key raw materials. One classic example in the Southeast is the extensive use of wood pulp in the production of paper. Other examples include the mining and processing of kaolin in middle Georgia; granite and marble extraction in north Georgia; the consumption of milk in the production of dairy products; and cattle, poultry, hogs, and other animals in meatpacking operations. Although access to raw materials is important to a relatively small number of manufacturing operations, you should document any advantages that the proximity of raw materials such as forest land, sand, gravel, or ore might offer.

Value-Added Manufactured Goods

Most production operations require the availability of critical value-added products. Every manufacturing plant consumes a variety of value-added products in the generation of its end products, which may be intermediate products in another production operation. One example is auto manufacturers who buy steel, glass, tires, plastic molded products, fabrics, electronic parts, fabricated metal parts, and other materials that are incorporated into vehicles assembled in their plants.

The fundamental choice for most companies is whether to locate close to markets or close to the sources of value-added manufactured goods. For some, such as auto makers, the cost of transporting the finished product to the customer is cheaper than the cost of transporting the parts to the assembly facility. These companies tend to seek sites for production facilities that are close to suppliers. With the continued growth of automobile production in the Southeast, much discussion has been given to attracting these value-added firms to supply materials to auto manufacturers in the region.

If you are seeking production facilities as one source of growth in your community, your community economic development action planning should document the production capacity of similar, or competing, manufacturers (at a four digit Standard Industrial Classification/SIC level) within one day's delivery time (about 100 to 300 miles) from your area. The size of the area from which your community can effectively draw value-added products is determined by the quality of the transportation services documented in the earlier discussion of market access.

Business and Professional Services

All businesses use a variety of business and professional services in the course of their operations. These include personnel supply services, accounting and financial management services, banking and insurance services, legal and medical services, protective and collection services, advertising and public relations services, clerical and mailing services, engineering and architectural services, laboratory services, computer and information processing services, management and economic consulting services, and equipment parts and repair services.

In large businesses, many services are provided by company employees. However, the smaller the company is, the greater the dependence on outside sources for these services. Consequently, an important location consideration for many smaller, owner-managed companies is whether these services are available and affordable. The selection of sites for major administrative headquarters and research facilities are influenced by the presence or absence of such key service providers as advertising and public relations firms, personnel supply firms, specialized law firms, and laboratories and testing services for research facilities.

Your community economic development action planning should identify local and regional sources of each of these types of services. It should highlight any special qualifications of these firms. In the absence of local sources, the action planning should describe where and how these services can be obtained. This part of your action planning should also identify, where appropriate, available passenger transportation services.

LABOR FORCE

Another resource consumed in the production of goods and the delivery of services is labor. Few facilities are totally automated, so the availability of a quality work force is important in any location decision. Three important aspects of the labor force in your community and area should be considered:

1. Worker availability

2. Skill level

3. Cost

Worker Availability

Potential employers are interested in being able to assemble and maintain a work force in the community. Although a high unemployment rate is undesirable from a community perspective, it is a potential asset in efforts to attract economic development investment.

Some of your community's labor force might lack basic literacy skills. Consequently, a community with an unemployment rate of 6 percent or less may have a potential labor shortage that will make their staff recruitment difficult or more expensive.

If your community's unemployment rate is higher than 6 percent, you can treat this as a location advantage if you can demonstrate that a significant share of available workers have work experience but have been displaced for various reasons. Albany, Georgia, is an excellent example of a community that used a high unemployment rate to their advantage. When the 1,000,000 square foot Firestone plant closed in the mid-80s, there was serious concern about whether Albany could find a replacement industry to put displaced workers back to work. An aggressive effort by the community, the Georgia Department of Labor (and their QuickStart training program), and other regional and state agencies who offered "one stop services" to displaced workers and potential new industries, drew the attention of Cooper Tire. These activities resulted in their move into the old Firestone facility and their hiring of a large portion of the previously out-of-work labor force in Albany.

It may be difficult for some communities to do what Albany did. However, if your area's unemployment rate is low, document an ability to draw workers from surrounding areas of higher unemployment or be prepared to accept this as a liability that you will have to address. In many counties in metropolitan areas, low unemployment is a major liability to attracting new businesses.

Skill Level

Although some types of facilities employ a work force that is predominantly unskilled, more and more require some semiskilled and skilled workers. Production workers and clerical workers are typically less mobile than their administrative and management counterparts.

To compete for manufacturing/production facilities or office-oriented businesses that employ significant numbers of semiskilled or skilled production or clerical workers, your community should document the presence of available workers or demonstrate the availability of workers with the skills needed by target businesses and/or the capacity the community has, or can obtain, to train unskilled workers to employer specifications. The availability of programs similar to Georgia's Quick-Start Program (a state supported program available to new or existing industry for "quickly" training employees or potential employees at the facility site) should be documented in your community economic development action planning.

Cost

All types of businesses are concerned about their labor costs, but this is most influential in the selection of sites for production-oriented facilities whose markets are highly cost competitive. For example, production labor costs are very important when siting a computer assembly plant because a facility should be able to manufacture units at a cost that is competitive with units produced in Taiwan, Korea, or China when transportation costs and tariffs are included.

To compete for facilities that are sensitive to labor costs, it is not sufficient to measure the average wage rate in the area.

The average wage rate is often influenced by local employers whose pay scales may be considered high, either because they reflect national labor contracts, or because the employers are buying stability and loyalty by paying more than other, similar firms. The critical question is: How much will the next employer opening a facility in the community have to pay to assemble a work force? Local wage surveys can provide an answer. This is an excellent project for local chambers of commerce to undertake on a regular basis.

But even this answer is not sufficient to determine the effective labor cost. You should also measure the relative productivity of local workers in comparison with regional and national norms. There are no reliable governmental figures that measure productivity differences among communities and regions. To generate defensible documentation about your community's productivity, turn to local employers whose companies have similar facilities in other locations. These companies frequently have internal information on the relative performance of their plants or offices, and they may be willing to share this information with you.

SITES

All new or expanded facilities require sites for their operations. The type and amount of space needed varies by type of activity. As the space required increases, this factor's importance also increases. Very large companies seeking locations for major facilities often prefer to assemble raw land and develop it themselves, as did General Motors and the Saturn production facility in Spring Hill, Tennessee.

Some investors are looking for site space with a completed structure that can be modified if necessary and occupied quickly. For communities seeking office-oriented businesses, the presence of a high office vacancy rate becomes a community asset rather than a liability, although it remains a liability to the owners until new businesses are attracted. In the same way, vacated manufacturing buildings can be an asset for communities seeking new manufacturers if those buildings are structurally sound and sufficiently flexible in design to accommodate a variety of production operations. Newly constructed speculative buildings typically meet this condition of flexibility.

Some businesses prefer to construct their own building or have it constructed to their specifications. Unless they have a long lead time, this means that they are looking for land that is ready for construction. For some companies, sites in industrial or office parks are desirable. For others, free-standing locations or downtown locations are better.

In your community's economic development action planning, acquire or assemble an inventory of the following available site space: vacant office space by class, size, general location, and cost (lease rates or sale price); vacant industrial sites/space separated by size of facility, nearness to transportation services, access to water and energy resources, and design characteristics; and, vacant, developable land ready for construction, segmented by zoning, size, and price. Document the cost for all of these types of sites and spaces and determine whether these costs are competitive with those found in other communities offering similar investment opportunities.

CAPITAL

Financial capital is a must in any new business or industry investment. The type and amount of capital needed are functions of the size and character of the investment, whether it be the expansion of an existing facility, the development of a new facility in the area by an established company, or the creation or acquisition of facilities to house a newly created business. The importance of locally provided capital tends to decline as the size of the corporation making the investment grows.

Large, established corporations normally use borrowed funds to finance the construction and equipping of new or expanded facilities. They typically have established relationships with several lenders and rarely consider the availability of local private sources of debt or equity financing in making location decisions. They are interested in subsidies that lower the cost of financing, such as various types of local tax abatements. These are especially important to firms who look for abatements to provide them an advantage in the marketplace.

Small to medium-size companies typically use a mix of debt and equity financing to cover the cost of constructing, equipping, and staffing new or expanded facilities. Some have established sources for borrowed funds and venture capital, but many do not. For those who do not, access to new sources of financing in a community where they might locate a new facility can be the difference between making and not making the investment. The presence of added debt financing, added equity investment or both, can be one of the most important advantages you have in attracting this type of company.

Many potential entrepreneurs considering the formation of new businesses should finance the early stages of their undertakings from their own resources or those of friends and relatives. Seed capital the initial equity financing needed to cover the costs associated with preliminary product service research business planning, and initial market testing, is typically needed in relatively small amounts but it tends to be the investment with the highest risk. Most venture capitalists are not interested at this early stage unless the idea has a strong new technology orientation and generates considerable excitement.

Communities with strong, private, informal networks of seed capital have an edge in attracting more new technology-based business formations. Some communities, such as those around major universities, such as Athens, Georgia, attempt to stimulate these new technology-based business formations artificially, usually with assistance from business incubators and educational facilities.

Your community economic development action planning should document the numbers, capacities, and performance characteristics of debt and equity financing sources that serve businesses in your community. Some of this information can be obtained from discussions with financial institutions and investors, but some of the qualitative judgments about the responsiveness of these sources and their willingness to work with entrepreneurs should come from those who seek and have sought funding in the community. Further, action planners need to document ways of securing access to debt, seed, and venture capital in the community. Variations in access to capital among businesses, based on the nature of their activities and size, should be documented. Because these sources of capital funding are unique, they should be evaluated separately in your community action planning.

INCENTIVES

The actions and policies of local and state governments directly affect both the ability of businesses to operate effectively in a community and the cost of those operations. Government investments in and maintenance of the physical infrastructure of the area the community's and state's secondary and post-secondary educational systems, and available health, safety, and recreational services can help create an environment conducive to profitable economic development operations. Governments can offer incentives designed to attract and retain businesses by lowering initial and/or ongoing costs.

To evaluate the governmental impact on your community's economic development potential, assess the level and quality of investments made in the following five areas:

1. Secondary and higher education

2. Transportation infrastructure (streets, roads, bridges, waterways, transportation terminals)

3. Public services (police, fire, health)

4. Water and wastewater treatment and distribution systems

5. Incentives offered to help businesses come to and operate profitably in your community.

What is the capacity and quality of these public resources in your community in comparison with those in competing communities?

TAXES AND FEES

The types and levels of taxes and fees to pay for services reduce the amount of profits retained by businesses and entrepreneurs who operate in the area. Assess the following types of local and state governmental policies that impose costs on business operations: regulatory policies that restrict the types of activities a business can undertake or that list rules under which it must operate; fees imposed on businesses to fund worker protection and benefit programs (worker compensation and unemployment benefits); business taxes; and personal taxes.

Data at an aggregate United States level are available for some of these measures, local or state sources can be used for others. Surveys of local business executives are an important source of information on these issues. Interpret statistical data carefully. For example, the average per capita tax burden imposed on residents of a state is an interesting statistic but it does not accurately measure economic development potential. Who pays the taxes is more important than the average tax amount paid in measuring the impact of the tax policy of specific types of business activity. The degree to which governments serving a community find the optimal balance between needed services and taxes to finance them is a major consideration in business location decisions.

QUALITY OF LIFE

Of all the factors affecting business location decisions, quality of life has received the most attention recently. Witness the increasing attention paid to this variable in publications such as *Site Location Magazine*. Recent work in measuring quality of life factors has moved to much more objective and quantifiable criteria such as traffic congestion, housing costs, costs and availability of medical services, and crime rates. Communities, by their very nature, represent diverse populations. Some of us are looking for a fast-paced life with fine restaurants, bars, nightclubs, concerts, and other forms of live entertainment. Others measure living quality in terms of the environment for raising a family: a strong moral environment, good neighborhoods and good neighbors, quality schools, low crime rates, access to sporting events, and outdoor recreation. Communities that meet one definition of quality can score poorly on others, so generalizations about a high quality of life are best given in an appropriate context. Most of the media assessments have emphasized factors important to professionals who populate new technology research and development facilities and professional service businesses such as advertising. Atlanta and other metro areas, coastal areas, and areas near cultural centers or major outdoor recreational facilities are the favored locations according to these assessments.

Some factors that affect quality of life have already been addressed; secondary schools, higher education facilities, local transportation systems that determine commuting times, and public recreational facilities. Other factors, such as natural resources (mountains, rivers, and lakes), weather, and geographic proximity to other points of interest, are inherited and must be accepted as is. Some factors are the natural result of the area's economic and social history, such as personal security, cost of living, and the quality and cost of housing.

The number of educational facilities and graduates, grade point averages, SAT scores, merit scholarships, graduate degree programs, graduate degrees awarded and other scores attempt to measure educational quality. All measure some aspect of the issue but none are complete measures of the quality or even the quantity of educational opportunities. They should be considered together.

Similar problems exist in efforts to measure the degree of personal security that one has in a community. Crime rates are often used, but there are potentially confusing differences in the ways these data are collected and reported. Public perception of security may be as good a measure as any.

Cost of living and cost of housing can be relatively accurate measures if the same elements are applied when comparisons are made. Climatological data, maintained by the Weather Bureau of the Commerce Department, can be a measure for most communities. Physical proximity to other communities and to recreational resources, such as beaches or mountains, is easily measured. There are several quality of life indexes that exist. Again, know what these indexes say about your community and be prepared to deal with its negative points and to build on its strengths.

SUMMARY

Many communities will experience substantial economic changes over the next decade. Those whose traditional employment base is in low-skilled manufacturing will feel the changes more intensely. Communities that understand the nature of the socioeconomic changes occurring around them and then act aggressively are likely to be much stronger from a community economic development and jobs creation perspective in 5 years than they are today.

We strongly believe that communities everywhere have problems that are, for the most part, solvable by local people. But to solve problems, you as a community must face up to them, accept them as weaknesses, and agree to an action plan for addressing and correcting them. Only then can your community take advantage of the opportunities created by the socioeconomic changes we have outlined. You can take specific community action that is well informed and well thought out. Action planning is the key to your success.

TIPS FOR STARTING A BUSINESS IN YOUR COMMUNITY

1. Provide a description and contact list for all of the forms, local and state tax requirements, zoning regulations, and related materials that a new business would need to start up.
2. Develop a list, or get it from another source, that describes education, training, and consulting services that a new business person might be interested in knowing about or attending and provide information on how to get on the mailing list of local, nearby, or regional continuing education programs.
3. Establish on-line access for the community and new businesses to gain information from the Internet and other information services.
4. Provide access to local banks, foundations, and investors that have seed capital for new businesses.
5. Establish a climate for information exchange between existing local businesses regarding the types of supplies, services, and materials needed locally that a new business might provide.
6. Provide office space, telecommunications, and clerical services at low cost to individuals interested in starting a new business.

   Comment: Currently we are unaware of any community that has marketed itself as having a favorable climate for new business start-ups. An aggressive community could promote its location; transportation access; telecommunications facilities; user-friendly governmental services; and cultural, educational, recreational, religious, and small town values that can become a haven for small business development. Good luck in your climate development efforts!

TIPS FOR EXPANDING AND/OR RETAINING
EXISTING BUSINESSES OR INDUSTRIES

Many communities traditionally have a business/industry appreciation day or week but what we are talking about is more than a one-time or annual event. We are suggesting a sincere, regular, and sustaining recognition, discussion and realization by the community of the impact made by existing or expanding businesses or industries.

1. Develop a climate that communicates We appreciate what you do for our community.
2. Set up regular meetings and communication opportunities (local cable and radio broadcasts, news articles, community events, breakfast or lunch roundtables, appreciation dinners) that explain, inform, and promote the impact and benefits of business and industry in the community. Note: information flows both ways and it can be positive or negative. For example, if an industry is violating an environmental regulation or is proposing to expand into unhealthy or undesirable ventures, the community is positioned to respond quickly and decisively.
3. Have someone or some organization in the community monitor the location, expansion, and service needs of existing businesses to enable the community to respond to these issues.
4. Discuss with new, as well as with existing businesses, what the community expects of a good neighbor contributing corporate citizens to the community. Too many knocks on the corporate doors for contributions, volunteers, and services can drive away existing businesses. Too few knocks on corporate doors to inquire about satisfaction and services can imply that the community is not interested. Work out a mutual agreement for communication and dialogue.

TIPS FOR KEEPING IN CONTACT
WITH POTENTIAL COMMERCIAL,
RETAIL, AND PRODUCTION OPERATIONS

In the new era of trying to recruit new commercial ventures it is *business as unusual*. Some communities are successful at landing a big fish, but most communities are directing their energies toward catching several small fish, developing a community climate that promotes existing business expansion, and promoting new business start-ups. Regardless of the approach to fishing for new businesses, what can be done?

1. Have available at the local library, college, or chamber of commerce access to up-to-date information and data sources. Maintain a contact list at the point of contact whether it be the chamber of commerce or some other location. Use spreadsheet software to develop a contact list including who called, when a call was made, what was asked, who gave the information, what was promised, when the promise was to be delivered (if something promised), should contact be called back, and who gave the community as a contact.

2. Provide local, regional, and statewide information with descriptions and discussions about what these data imply.

3. Have access to and be able to provide a listing or inventory of available land, buildings, resources, and investors interested in development.

4. Develop a community strategy for telling your story to potential investors or developers. You may have only enough resources to work through statewide developers, if so, make sure they have current information about your community. You may want to make your own contacts via newspapers, trade shows, and international networks, if so, have your presentation developed and streamlined to professionally tell your story.

CHAPTER 8

Funding and Support for Community Economic Development

We do not see funding and support as the most important activity in conducting community economic development. In fact, we have often observed community groups getting "stalled out" over their discussion about how they need money to do this project and that project, becoming frustrated over not being able to cite readily available sources of support, and disbanding and going home.

We have postponed the discussion of funding and support until now, although we have been encouraged to put this earlier in the book so that readers have an idea of where they can get money to do the necessary activities, programs, and projects. Our reason for postponement is discussed in this chapter and in Chapter 9.

We do not deny that funding, resources, support, in-kind or donated labor, and volunteer involvement are all necessary to carry out successful community economic development activities. We do however believe that there is an optimum time for discussing funding and support, and it is not the FIRST thing a group needs to do when thinking about their vision for community improvement and change. For discussion purposes we are saying it should be the LAST item discussed in the community economic development process. We have listed other factors, from our perspective, that should come before seeking funding such as, educating and organizing your volunteers and community leaders; inventorying your community resources in terms of recreation potential, historic, and scenic sites; putting in place some networking and telecommunications resources and facilities; and leveraging and promoting existing resources such as buildings, sites, businesses and industries, local skills, and educational facilities for community economic development.

Once the community knows itself and discusses its resources, strengths, and weaknesses it is then ready to enter into action planning. Action planning, as described in Chapter 2 and Figures 2.1 and 2.2, involves designing strategies for achieving the community vision. This process involves understanding the issues, problems, dilemmas, and possible options for implementation. Information and education about issues, dilemmas, and concerns put volunteers and leaders in a better position to understand the magnitude of resources needed.

Now we are ready to examine what funding and support resources are required for implementing community improvements or change. We recognize that this process may not be so linear, and some of these discussions may go on simultaneously. Part of our role in working with communities is to not let discussions about money and funding get in the way of first thinking about "what should be done." Communities that focus on "what can be done" often find funding and support from a variety of agencies once they clarify the goal, task, or project.

WHERE DO WE BEGIN?

The beginning point is to determine how widely accepted and how much of the community was involved in the development of the community vision? If the community vision is accepted by a cross section of the community and if there are multiple ways the vision impacts many different community groups, then the task of getting people to help support improvements and change will be relatively easy. By the same analysis, if the vision represents a narrow perspective within the community, broad based support will be difficult to obtain.

Look Within the Community for Support

We have observed active and successful communities making an internal inventory of who is interested and who has the time or resources to help get the job done. For example, part of the community vision for Colquitt, Miller County, Georgia, was to improve the visibility and safety of downtown after dark. They determined they had a need for street lighting. An initial plan required 18 street lights. The community responded with 28 donations of $1,000 each for the purchase, wiring, and installation of the lights. The additional 10 streetlights have been erected along downtown access streets, primarily based upon community requests and initial action planning.

Crawfordville, Taliaferro County, Georgia, utilized nearby resources of the University of Georgia to make an inventory of their historic homes and downtown buildings that will be helpful in writing grants for historic district designations as well as for improvements in the downtown business district.

Blakely, Early County, Georgia, has designated a local theater as one of the buildings on the downtown square that the community would like to improve and possibly restore for either business or community meeting site purposes. The local chamber of commerce has applied for a grant from the Municipal Electric Authority of Georgia (MEAG) for $5,000 for the group to identify the full range of improvements, costs, and benefits to the community. Part of this study involves a broad cross section of people in the community to help establish priorities, needs, and resources for the renovations.

Representatives at the Georgia Farm Bureau have been active in promoting the development of local community bed and breakfast business operations. They have held workshops and conferences about how to start and operate a bed and breakfast inn. Additional help, in the form of workshops and consultations, is available to entrepreneurs from the Small Business Development Program located at the University of Georgia. Similar programs are available in other states.

It is incumbent upon the community to establish their vision, identify local resources, involve persons and agencies in action planning, suggest alternatives for implementation, and take their plan to local residents for assistance. In addition to looking for local support, the community may want to leverage their support to locate resources from state, regional, or local agencies. Support may also be available from multi-state regional or federal agencies.

Engage Your Neighbors
(Adjoining Counties and/or Cities)

One of the things we have tried to promote in our focus on community economic development activities is the development of an energy source of individuals and groups that share similar interests across county boundaries. At our Community Economic Development Planning (CEDP) institutes we have invited representative teams from adjoining counties to experience the action learning event. As they share action plans they notice similar interests in transportation, such as highway development; alternative agriculture products, such as peanuts, cotton, timber, onions, sunflowers, etc.; and tourism events, such as developing coordinated festival tours through southeast Georgia. Even when we took requests for CEDP from counties and cities scattered throughout the state, they found mutual interests, such as vegetable production from Stewart county for the farmers' market in the city of Decatur, near Atlanta.

The tourism subcommittee, representing the Council of Economic Development Organizations (CEDO) Region 11 that participated in the 1994–95 Georgia Academy for Economic Development, has written a grant to secure funding for the preparation of marketing materials for coordinated regional events. They promoted such things as festivals, cultural events, and recreation resources to be used during the 1996 Summer Olympics and future visitations.

Another group of individuals in northwest Georgia (i.e., participants in CEDP-IV January 1995) met with local and regional leaders to coordinate the development of a regional agriculture/education facility. The facility will be adapted to accommodate agricultural events such as displays, festivals, and shows for residents in a six county area. In addition, the facility will be adapted to accommodate meetings and retreats for existing businesses and for individuals wishing to begin new business ventures. Local funds have been identified for making construction modifications to existing buildings and for a new building should the need arise. It is anticipated that private investors will support this development that will benefit and service residents in a multi-county area.

Identify Resources for Regional In-state and Multi-state Projects

In-state regional organizations like Regional Development Commissions and multi-state agencies like the Tennessee Valley Authority (TVA), the Appalachian Regional Commission (ARC) and the Four Corners Development Commission have been formed to facilitate economic development in almost every area of the United States. Multijurisdiction councils of government (COGs) and other arrangements like Regional Educational Service Agencies (RESAs) offer benefits and services that would not ordinarily be available to individual local entities. Community and multi-county economic development groups can often obtain consultation, technical assistance, and funding support for economic development activities. Most agencies require a comprehensive plan, report, or document (e.g., vision, action plan, and local commitment for implementation) that specifies what is going to happen, to whom, and for what results (i.e., outcomes, value added.).

Regional planning agencies in Georgia have staff members with expertise to assist communities with community planning, historic preservation, tourism, marketing, and grant writing. In addition they are knowledgeable of the grants and resources available from the state and from several federal sources.

Another source of assistance for identifying potential grants are the development offices of major colleges and universities in your area or state. At these offices, individuals can help you identify potential grants for a variety of projects from multistate (regional), federal, corporate, and nonprofit sectors.

Recently the designation of empowerment zones and enterprise communities by the federal government has made monies available to selected cities and communities for economic improvements. Specifically, the empowerment zones provide funds and matching monies to improve education, training, and job-finding assistance for communities.

Research the Foundations

One particularly fruitful area of support comes from the foundations in both the corporate and nonprofit sectors. For example, the Kellogg Foundation has a long history of supporting community economic development ventures that relate to improving health care delivery in rural areas. Another foundation, the Ford Foundation, is currently assisting international communities in improving their community development infrastructure.

Also, it is important to research which foundations restrict their assistance to rural communities in specific states and for specific populations. Some foundations have been set up just for a particular county or borough, or for a specific purpose such as the provision of college scholarships for residents of a particular Ohio county by the Pepsi Foundation. Another example is a local foundation in Maxey, Georgia, which will pay the tuition for children of local residents who want to attend the University of Georgia. There may be other individual foundations available for local community economic development.

Develop Your Own Funding

Community development corporations (CDC's) are locally designed funding mechanisms to support community economic development. Individuals or small groups combine their resources to establish a reservoir of funds that are available to local entrepreneurs to support their activities. Payback of funds usually involves a lower interest rate for the loan and monies are maintained in the fund accessible to other local entrepreneurs. CDC's usually establish themselves as a 501(c)(3) nonprofit corporation. Some CDC's are designed specifically to provide training and employment for unemployed people in the community.

Examples

Thumbody Enterprises, of Caro, Michigan, used low-income residents to assist in weatherizing homes in the rural thumb area of Michigan. A community action agency offered a weatherization program which included educational training on energy conservation. To complement the program, a separate corporation, Thumbody Enterprises, was established. The business manufactured low cost insulation products such as storm windows, storm doors, and weatherstripping to sell to rural residents. This community business provided employment to previously hard core unemployed people who were trained through a skills development program.

Latino Economic Development Corporation, in Washington, D.C., grew out of the frustration and discontentment among neighborhood residents. This prompted people to organize a CDC to address their economic needs. Since the majority of these residents are immigrants who encounter language barriers and employment problems, they have resorted to establishing informal micro-enterprises. To respond to the growing micro-enterprise movement in the community, the Latino CDC formed a credit union and a micro-enterprise loan fund. These activities are aimed at providing financial resources and business training to existing and potential microentrepreneurs so that they can eventually operate in the formal economy. The CDC is exploring the creation of a vendors' mall where they can market their products.

Appalachian Mountain High, is a private, non-profit venture capital firm created to back entrepreneurs to spur job creation. Founded in 1968 as an outgrowth of various Great Society antipoverty efforts, the Kentucky Highlands Project was conceived as a catalyst for promoting local economic development. Kentucky Highlands focused the majority of its efforts on job creation mainly by investing in existing or start-up companies. What distinguishes Kentucky Highlands from traditional venture capital firms is that it doesn't pocket the profits. Instead, all of the earnings are reinvested into backing more entrepreneurs who will create even more jobs in the community. Although Kentucky Highlands has had its share of failures, it can take credit for the net creation of 1,800 new jobs that annually generate some $20 million in direct income.

INDIVIDUAL COMMUNITY APPROACH

We are aware of a number of communities throughout the country that have decided they must do their own fund-raising and generate their own support for community economic development activities. Volunteers and local leaders have identified a disorienting dilemma that affects everyone in the community in some way. Their first attempt at securing support and funding is focused on local sources. Utilizing local sources for leverage they contact other funding agencies and organizations. In some communities local sources have been substantial, for example, one community in southwest Georgia was able to secure $1 million from a community foundation to finance the renovation of an old hotel. Other communities have used contributions from residents and merchants to demonstrate local support or commitment to a project or idea. Funding agencies use local commitment as a gauge of community support before investing their resources in projects.

Example: Wrightsville, Johnson County, Georgia

The Chamber of Commerce Executive Director and volunteers in Wrightsville, Johnson County, Georgia, had described and taken pictures of most of their many community economic development projects from May 1992 through December 1993. They had put on festivals (Community HeeHaw), sponsored clean up downtown events, renovated their train depot, developed a downtown and community walking tour, recruited businesses for downtown, worked to locate a fast food store in the community, and began explorations for a small hotel or motel. They were in need of an infusion of support and funding for additional projects to assist in their community development efforts. In short, they begged and borrowed paint, lumber and landscaping materials, and they had just about exhausted their volunteers in doing clean up and related projects.

What they did next is a possible marketing tool for generating funding and support at the next level. The Chamber Executive Director put together a notebook with visuals and written explanations of all of their projects. The presentation team of the Executive Director and two volunteers drove to Atlanta and began making presentations to statewide economic developers. What was different about their presentation? The community didn't ask for money! What they did was tell the different groups this is what we have been doing with local monies and donated time. This is what we have on our action plan agenda for the next 2 years, and this is what we hope to achieve. Statewide developer reactions included comments such as, "Well how much money do you need from us?" The developers were the first to ask! And, they asked how much money the community needed! This is a change in strategy from begging for support and dollars without a plan or implementation strategy. The plan worked. The group received no grants or direct cash outlays as a consequence of the meeting, but they did make statewide developers aware of who they were and what they were doing. The meeting did open doors to other resources and contacts. One contact in particular, related to the location of a fast food franchise in the downtown area because of their efforts to positively promote the community. The franchisee was impressed with the community's support and tenacity in selling their community. Maybe this approach will work for you in your community.

SUMMARY

There is no single formula for securing funding for community economic development projects. Each community will have to look at their action planning strategy and try to match their vision with one or more funding sources. The difficulty with this matching process is like trying to shoot through several windows. Sometimes community goals don't exactly match the funding sources available. The bottom line to securing funding is like all bottom lines. It really depends on how imaginative and creative you are in matching funding sources to your project. Our experience is that funding will be a result of hard work and diligence, not blind luck, although we have seen some successful "blind hogs" who have stumbled upon an "acorn" occasionally. Following are some tips and suggestions from several communities who have been successful in securing funding.

TIPS ON WRITING PROPOSALS:

There are three distinct phases for preparing a proposal for funding: preliminary planning and research; effective proposal writing; and proposal follow-up (Economic Development Diges, 1994; Rural Information Center, 1994).

Preliminary Planning and Research

1. Identify a need.
2. Determine what, as specifically and clearly as you can, your community will apply for.
3. Analyze agencies, organizations, and foundations for a potential match between your need and their willingness to fund or support.
4. Read the request for proposal (RFP) or description (General Guidelines) very carefully. Call for explanations if you do not understand details and follow the RFP or guidelines very closely.

Effective Proposal Writing

1. Keep your proposal short, simple, and to the point.
2. Clearly state your problems, goals, objectives, and explain how your proposal will address or resolve these issues.
3. Set realistic goals or objectives and specify how your activities, program or proposal, will be carried out to resolve these issues.
4. Follow the RFP or guidelines for proposals format; change your format to accommodate theirs. Proposal readers should be able to follow your proposal, plans, and programs within their format.
5. Make sure your budget is on target and can be easily related to what you plan to do with your proposal.
6. Explain your evaluation processes clearly. The concern is how well the funding agency will be able to determine how many goals and objectives your community has achieved.
7. Explain how you will meet required deadlines. Be

specific and clear about what your proposal or plan will do to accommodate and meet deadlines.

8. Review your proposal to make sure it meets requirements and clearly specifies activities and budgets. Do not forget to include adequate review time in the proposal development process.
9. Submit your proposal on time to the specified agent or agency.

Proposal Follow-up

1. Obtain a receipt or record of your proposal being received on time by the specified agent or agency.
2. Stay in contact with the agency to determine if your proposal is accepted. If unsuccessful gather as much information as possible on what did not meet agency guidelines/RFP. Get specific information so you do not make these mistakes again; if successful confirm start dates and timelines. Be agreeable but cautious as you revise the scope of work and budget of the proposal.
3. Begin the project or program and meet your timelines as agreed. Keep the project monitor informed of project as required.
4. If appropriate, identify needs for additional project funding and the availability of future funding from this organization.

TIPS FOR SECURING FUNDING AND SUPPORT
FOR COMMUNITY ECONOMIC DEVELOPMENT

1. Decide what your community vision is first. What does the community want to improve or change in the next few months or couple of years?
2. Identify your community priorities for action and funding needs.
3. Design your action plan for these priorities.
4. Obtain support locally for getting these priorities accomplished.
5. Get organized and put together your story about community economic development.
6. Tell your story to different agencies who might have funding and support resources; ask them to help you identify your shared visions and needs.
7. Include foundations of both corporate and nonprofit agencies as groups with which you share information about your community economic development action plans and strategies.
8. Learn grant writing skills. Seek help from regional planning agencies and staffs, universities, and nonprofit agencies.
9. Follow up with your initial contacts. Inform them of what has been accomplished since you last talked.
10. Don't give up!

TIPS ON FUNDING RESOURCES

This information is from the Rural Information Center (RIC), a good contact for you in your community economic development activities. RIC Phone number is 1-800-633-7701. Publications that might be helpful to communities seeking funding possibilities for community economic development include:

1. Federal Grants and Contract Weekly. Arlington, VA.: Capitol Publications
2. Federal Register. Washington, D.C.: Office of the Federal Register
3. Foundations and Corporate Grants Alert. Alexandria, VA: Capital Publications
4. Foundation Giving Watch. Washington, D.C.: Taft Corporation
5. Foundation Giving Index Quarterly. New York: Foundation Center
6. Distance Learning Funding Sources, "Jesus Ricardo Lucero and Others" (Pennsylvania: Mansfield University, 1992), 25 pp. ERIC 358813.
7. Bingham, E. D., Hill, E. W., and White, S. B. (Eds.) (1990). *Financing Economic Development*. Newbury Park, CA: Sage Publications.

CHAPTER 9

Using a Different Approach for Community Economic Development

COMMUNITY VISION

Communities that are successful in organizing and carrying out community economic development ideas and projects, involve a diverse and broad cross section of local residents. The process we use in getting this broad and diverse community group to take into account all of their different perspectives about what should or shouldn't happen in the community is our *visioning exercise*. It is important, in this visioning exercise, that all voices in the group be heard. This is especially critical in communities where, in the past, all voices have not been heard. We see this visioning exercise as a technique to get information and ideas about everyone's issues, concerns, and dreams for the future.

We have all members of community groups share their views in a visual format. We ask everyone to do several things in the visioning exercise.

- Think about their community in the future, say 2 to 5 years from today.
- What would they take a visitor to see in their community of the future?
- What does the community look like?
- Participants each prepare a drawing of their vision of their community in the future.
- In small groups (four to eight people) participants share with each other what their drawings represent or illustrate.

- As a small group, participants incorporate *all* of their ideas into a collective vision.
- Each small group then discusses their vision for the future with the other participants.
- A global vision for the future, developed by the entire group, is produced by looking at the drawings for what's similar, what's different, and what's been omitted.
- In addition to the visual presentations, notes and comments made by each presentation have been written on flip charts and reviewed by the group.
- A general discussion by the group summarizes the factors that make up the total group vision for the future.
- Groups then use their visuals and descriptions as slogans, logos, and marketing tools to inform and rally broad community support.
- The larger community then has the opportunity to: accept add to, modify, enhance, or change the vision of their future community.
- Periodically the group reviews the vision, making modifications as needed, depending upon what ideas or projects have been accomplished or redirected.
- For sustained community economic development the most important factor in the visioning exercise is the periodic review (the Action Learning/Planning Model, Figure 2.1).

THE CONYERS/ROCKDALE
COUNTY GATEWAY PROJECT

The Conyers/Rockdale County Chamber of Commerce, in the spring of 1992, invited the Institute of Community and Area Development (ICAD) from the University of Georgia to help facilitate the development of a strategic plan for economic development. This plan was to be a 5-year community economic development work program for the chamber of commerce. This work program would provide the framework for the chamber to move toward an increased emphasis on assuming a leadership role in the community for economic development activities. That plan was formulated over a long series of meetings and was presented to the chamber board at a retreat in November of 1992.

This 5-year strategic plan provided some new directions for chamber involvement in the overall betterment of the Conyers/Rockdale community. One area of the strategic plan was a concern over how the chamber could increase the aesthetics of the community for economic development purposes. The plan suggested the instigation of a gateway project that would focus on improving the appearance of the main street of the community, the I-20 corridor (ICAD, 1994).

In October 1993, ICAD held the first public meeting to begin the process of the Conyers Rockdale I-20 Corridor Project. From this meeting design criteria were suggested that provided the basis for the involvement of the environmental design students and the further refinement of these design criteria ideas and suggestions through other meetings with the public and chamber of commerce by ICAD faculty and staff.

Applied Visioning Exercise

The first step in the process involved conducting a visual analysis and inventory of the existing conditions along the 8 1/2-mile I-20 corridor that is within Rockdale County. The unique features of the corridor, which include frontage roads to the north and south, a diverse mix of land uses, and a rapidly developing region, all contribute to the visual clutter along I-20. Numerous billboards, signs, and flags compete for the attention of motorists traveling through the county. A lack of maintenance of the land between the interstate and the frontage roads is evident in the eroding bare spots, the rusting and broken fencing, the abundance of weeds, and the amount of roadside litter. The four interchanges are nondescript and uninviting. In essence, there is nothing about the I-20 corridor, identified as "Main Street" Conyers Rockdale County, that reflects the many positive characteristics of the community.

Other Communities

Information was collected from other communities with similar conditions. States such as North Carolina and Florida have implemented statewide roadside wildflower planting programs. Many communities, such as Research Triangle Park and Chapel Hill, North Carolina, have implemented master-planned roadside landscaping projects to define and enhance their community image. Closer to home, in the Atlanta metro areas, the Georgia Department of Transportation has landscaped large portions of highway roadside within the I-285 perimeter. The City of Columbus, through a combination of private and public funding, has installed landscaping at six key interchange gateways with more in the planning stages. The successes and failures of these and other projects provided valuable information for the I-20 Corridor Project.

Stakeholder's Meeting

Property owners along the I-20 corridor were identified and invited to attend a stakeholder's meeting in October 1993. The purpose of the meeting was to envision positive changes along the corridor. Slides of the existing conditions were presented at this meeting as well as slides showing how other communities had responded to similar problems and opportunities. After the slide presentation the group was asked to create a vision for the corridor, list possible barriers to change, and identify what it would take to implement their vision. These comments were collected and formed the basis of both the design criteria and the action plan presented in the report.

Design Criteria

The responses from the initial stakeholder's meeting were worked into a set of design criteria in the form of guidelines.

These guidelines helped shape the conceptual designs and continue to guide the design process as the project moves into the construction design phase.

Design Approach Statement: The I-20 corridor has been identified by the community as Main Street Conyers Rockdale County. The 8-1/2 mile section of a six-lane interstate bisects the county and includes four interchanges, each a gateway opportunity. The corridor is characterized by multiple abutting land uses, separated from the interstate by two-lane frontage roads, mixed chain-link and hog wire fences, as well as various shrubs, weeds, and trees (some deliberate, others volunteer), all of which contribute to visual chaos. Redesign of the visual elements along the corridor should stress uniformity and continuity to create a memorable positive image of the community. The following were design guidelines for the Gateway Project:

1. Landscape improvements should address issues of continuity, uniformity, and coherence along both the interstate and frontage road right-of-ways.

2. Landscape improvements should create areas of visual interest and should focus attention on these areas.

3. Each intersection is a gateway associated with a particular theme. Designs, such as sculpture, can be used to reflect these themes. The themes for each intersection are as follows: Sigman Road — Community Gateway; West Avenue — Olde Towne Gateway; Highway 138 — Olympic Gateway; and Salem Road — Industrial Gateway.

4. Attention should be given to the fencing and lighting.

5. Plant massings should not obstruct views.

6. Designs should provide seasonal interest.

7. Design should conform to Department of Transportation design guidelines.

Conceptual Design

Students in two design studio classes in the School of Environmental Design at the University of Georgia used the corridor as a class project. Given the design criteria mentioned above the students were asked to develop conceptual plans for the corridor. Midway through the class projects, members of the chamber of commerce participated in a critique of these preliminary designs. After several weeks of refinements to the plans, members of the chamber were invited to return to the School of Environmental Design and participate in the classes' final presentations where they selected six projects for special recognition. These conceptual plans were presented during a public meeting in March 1994, and the public was asked to respond to their concepts. The comments were used to shape the final conceptual drawings.

Illustrative Character Sketches

ICAD faculty used the responses from the second public meeting to articulate a coherent concept for the I-20 corridor. The concept was illustrated in a series of color drawings which showed possible design concepts for the corridor. The purpose of these drawings was to illustrate the character of possible design solutions for the I-20 corridor. They were numbered in sequence, beginning at the county line and travelling eastbound along I-20. Each drawing depicted a section of the corridor.

Implementation Plan

Each key issue identified at the stakeholders' meeting was addressed in the implementation plan with suggestions for action as well as references to landscape contractors and possible funding resources. Breaking the implementation plan into single issues created tasks of manageable size. The next step for the chamber was to prioritize elements of the plan and begin work on those of highest priority. The Gateway Project is illustrative of what a community can do if there is a desire to accomplish a task.

STRATEGIES FOR SUCCESS

Through our work with leaders and volunteers in community after community, we have identified issues and strategies important to communities achieving their vision for community economic development.

Dealing with Money

"How much will it cost?" "Who is going to pay for this?" "We don't have enough money in our existing budget to cover these ideas!" How many times have you heard these and related questions or statements about the availability of funds or resources to accomplish a task or project? Resources, funding, in-kind support, and volunteers or paid staff to get the task completed are basic concerns of residents wanting to try something new. Our experience in working with communities is that if we can get the group to put off dealing with the money issues until the last activity, we get creative ideas and interesting ways for getting a project started. We have observed that groups that are successful do not use the lack of money as an excuse for doing nothing. Instead, they share ideas, discuss issues, think about creative ways of getting the job done, and then they explore a **variety** of ways to implement and fund their vision, i.e., project.

Asking for Assistance within the Community

Groups that check first within the community for ideas, assistance, and resources before asking outsiders for their investments and commitments seem to have a better idea of their capacity for change. A community group in Wrightsville, Johnson County, Georgia used their action plan, accomplishments, and proposed projects as a tool to communicate with local elected officials, residents, and existing community groups. They were successful in getting additional volunteers to help with cleaning up alley ways, painting a downtown mural, locating plants on the sidewalks, establishing a walking tour downtown, and renovating the train depot for offices. They wrote a report of each project activity and listed volunteers and time invested and developed a photo notebook. These reports and notebooks were the communication tools used within the county. Representatives of the Wrightsville, Johnson County group made several presentations to statewide developers and used these same reports and notebooks to document their activities and describe local support for projects. Available assistance from outside sources was identified and secured based upon their action plan and documentation of what local residents had already committed.

Involving Local Residents in the
Plan/Implementation Process

Soliciting participation, assistance, ideas, and commitment from local residents is basic to getting acceptance for community change. Successful communities use a variety of strategies for involvement. One community meets regularly in roundtable sessions with the many boards, associations, elected officials, and the general public to update progress on implementation and to bring into the discussion other needs, projects, and happenings. Another community uses a monthly chamber of commerce newsletter to keep the individuals informed and to hold public meetings to discuss issues and suggested projects or needs. Another community has installed Free Net, a type of telecommunications community bulletin board, provided by a consortium of the local phone company and other interested parties, to inform residents of community happenings and things of interest. Some creative leadership development groups automatically plug their members into community activities and groups so that they can be another energy source of ideas and support for community change development activities. There are a variety of techniques and strategies for involving a broad base of residents, leaders, and locally elected officials in the plan/implementation process. The desired outcome from broad based involvement is more ideas for change and more support by the group and the community at the implementation stage.

Being Persistent in Asking for Help

Asking for help is not the same as begging. Community groups need to keep in mind that people will help with community change, if they are asked. Direct personal contact is a better strategy than an informal solicitation letter. Communities that have a successful track record in getting individuals, agencies, organizations, or groups to provide some type of assistance or help are the ones that ask for assistance, not just one time, but several times. The first contact, project, or request may not be a convenient one for someone to participate in. Don't give up! Contact them again, and again, and be persistent! One community wanted their elected officials to participate in their planning/implementation process so much that they began holding their meetings in city hall so it was very convenient for elected officials and others to attend their sessions.

Keeping Ideas Alive

In meetings and personal conversations we are often confronted with naysayers or people who say no before thinking about the topic or issue. One of the ground rules we use for meetings is to request that the group not discuss or criticize an idea until all participants have had the opportunity to share their notions about an issue. Next we ask the group to develop

criteria for reviewing each idea suggested, and then we systematically discuss each topic for both strengths and weaknesses.
What individuals and groups fail to do is listen to everyone's
ideas, think about all of the ideas, systematically review the
ideas, and then make suggestions for how to proceed with the
best ideas. There is a time within any community change process for individuals and groups to consider wild and crazy notions to stimulate their creativity and get outside of the "we
can't do this because we never did it before" mentality.

One community had a wild notion of building a walkway
out into a marsh for people to enjoy their natural swamp. Today this is one of the most used attractions for adult visitors in
their community. Visitors can view plants, wildlife, and water
creatures from an elevated walkway that doesn't require a boat
or other equipment.

Another community has promoted the special taste of
their sweet Vidalia onions and has even registered this product
in seventeen counties in Georgia. The culture of barbeque is so
active in one location in the state that this community hosts the
Big Pig Jig and draws thousands of people during one week and
two weekends. We venture that most community festival ideas
began as a wild and crazy notion that caught the attention of
residents and with some hard work have blossomed into successful community economic development projects.

Finding Many Ways to Reach Goals

Community groups and individuals that believe there are
many ways to accomplish what they want to achieve seem to
have more flexibility in involving residents and in getting the
job done. Keeping options open and promoting different ideas
for community change tends to be the priority for the 1990s.
One community, in preparing for the 1996 Olympics, involved
a broad cross section of the county, faculty and students at a
university, and local expertise in a partnership. The partnership
suggested how they wanted the interstate and bridges to be
more user friendly and beautiful. Residents described the con-

cept they wanted, faculty and students listened, and local expertise in the form of elected officials and environmentalists described both the potential and limits for development. The partnership went to work. Students, with faculty supervision,
visited, took pictures, and began to produce a variety of visuals
that might meet their requirements.

After several meetings with the partnership, the final product was an array of sketches, drawings, and renderings that offered a variety of ways to achieve user friendly and beautiful
interstate and exit ramp access. All of the partnership members
suggested many different ways to achieve the goal. The project
was a win/win situation where the community got to participate in describing their needs, faculty and students got to work
on a real live project, and community resources had input into
the possibilities and environmental limits.

Knowing What Others Know about the Community

The perceptions that others have about your community
can be both a strength and a weakness. Positive images about a
community such as free of trash and litter, a neat and well-kept
downtown and shopping areas, a safe community for residents,
affordable housing, accessible and affordable health care, and a
long list of other factors produce good feelings about a community. In some states (including Georgia) statewide developers
have information, data, and visuals that display land use and
development features (e.g., acres, paved roads, rail access, air-
ports, water resources, soil conditions, utilities to specific locations including industrial parks/facilities, telecommunications,
and a host of other information). It is important for the community to review and up-date this information on a periodic
basis and to spend time discussing the strengths of your county
with statewide developers so they are informed of your capacities, potential, and plans for future development.

A community group could use the updating process as
both a learning activity and a "get to know" statewide developers function for residents. Participants could learn about

their county and the services offered by statewide developers and begin to fit together local and statewide efforts for community economic development.

Dressing for Success

As mentioned previously, perceptions about communities are evident every time someone drives into and stops in your county. How visitors are greeted by: welcome signs to the community; service employees at restaurants, gas stations, shops; and manufacturing operations, creates an image. The question becomes, is your community dressed for success? Are the streets free of litter and debris? Are service employees positive greeters and helpful to visitors? Would visitors want to come back to your community?

Communities that have taken the time to work together to present their best profile are dressed for success. They have cleaned up downtown and rural roadsides. They have trained their service employees and people who come in contact with the public to be hospitable and helpful. They have made their community accessible and responsive to visitors and have worked hard at presenting a climate of hospitality, safety, and prosperity. For example, Hawkinsville, Georgia, has been successful at presenting a clean downtown with shops and store fronts that reflect a coordinated theme and design. Off street parking is available, signage is uncluttered and pleasing, streets and buildings are well marked, traffic flow is manageable with one-way streets east and west through town on the major highways, tourist attractions (e.g., the harness track) are easily found and, a signage theme (i.e., Historic Hawkinsville with the surrey and driver emblem) is presented at all entrances to the county.

Working on Problem Areas
(Ugly Babies) in the Community

Have residents by themselves, or with the assistance of others, committed to work on their ugly babies? An ugly baby is the single location or section of town with abandoned houses or buildings, a vacant lot with trash and debris, the industrial park that is cluttered with vehicles or building materials, or unkempt building sites. Currently, statewide developers in Georgia offer to make visits to counties or communities like they were a business owner or someone starting a business to critique the area. In short, they are looking for ugly babies that might prevent someone from relocating to the community. Also, they are looking for things in the community that might draw new businesses or start-ups.

Learning from Others' Successes and Failures

At a recent meeting in Athens, Georgia, a community group was talking about their visit to Cleveland. We were impressed that the group had traveled all the way to Ohio. They informed us that they visited Cleveland, Tennessee, to look at an agricultural and education facility they wanted to copy and develop in north Georgia. The group had also visited similar complexes in Georgia, Florida, and Alabama. Further, they had requested video tapes from as far away as California, Texas, and Kentucky. Clearly, the group was learning about similar facilities in other states and gathering information about what did and did not work.

Not Letting Past Experiences Dictate

Community groups that involve a broad cross section of participants (i.e., not just the usual suspects) tend to try new, challenging, and creative ways for promoting community economic development. People have good ideas and when they are encouraged to share this information, the entire group benefits. Sometimes new ideas are not anymore innovative than is the current practice. However, if new ideas and approaches are discouraged the group will never know how good they could have been.

One way we help community groups identify new ap-

proaches is to spend time discussing and clarifying the problem
or issue without automatically assuming that problem #1 has
answer #1 connected to it. We try to get the group to separate
the problem from solutions. We then have the group generate a
range of possible solutions, and then have the group evaluate
which solutions are practical, achievable, and politically possible, and then examine their cost. This process tends to identify
new or creative approaches rather than assume that a given
problem or issue has a solution attached to it.

Working Together in the Community

Each community has many boards, groups, associations,
and departments working toward the same goal of maintaining
and/or improving the quality of life in the city, town, community, or county. Sometimes these groups support each other
such as the School Board and the Highway Department (e.g.,
we need safe roads to transport our school children) and sometimes they compete with each other (e.g., the public library and
public schools each want to develop a learning environment
within their facility). It is very apparent to community visitors
when community groups cannot work together. Successful
community groups have developed the capacity to listen to
conflicting points of view and to use this energy to find mutually acceptable solutions. It is also evident to visitors when
groups are successful in working together and are willing to
share credit or give credit and recognition to a larger organization (e.g., the chamber of commerce or community organization).

Specifying What Success Means to the Community

Communities that share a vision of change or improvement, work together in implementing strategies and share recognition for accomplishments, can identify what success means
to them. In some communities, it is to bring everyone together

for a community meeting or to make a major decision regarding recreation facilities or to complete an action plan that many groups can support. Communities that take the time to listen to residents, look for new and creative ideas to problem-solve, and get broad based support for implementation have little trouble in identifying what success means to them. Success is their part of the vision for the community.

Recipe for a Community Economic Development Stew

There are many factors or ingredients to put into the stew, but each community defines the recipe. This is to say that each community uses what it has or what it can develop. Each community may have recreation resources, but one may have mountains, and the other may have coastal marshes. Both communities can market and develop their resources, but they will be promoting different aspects of recreation.

Communities must also be willing to change the recipe to fit local needs. For example, the city of Thomaston, in Upson County, Georgia, has been able to obtain funding to build an airport and terminal. They wanted the airport to support the transportation needs of existing business and industry as well as for locating future industries in the county. Interest and support for an airport in a nearby community may not have received funding because there was not as great a need.

STUDIES OR ACTION: THE CHICKEN OR THE EGG DILEMMA

Those communities that have good ideas, work to gain commitment and support, and look for creative ways to implement projects have been successful. One quick way to slow down or kill an activity is for the group to put off working on a project while it is studied. Do not misunderstand our point! We believe in studies and collecting data or information for decision making but for a group to stop its planning and discussions about community economic development projects while it conducts one or more studies can sidetrack a good idea.

For years, residents and leaders in Hawkinsville, Georgia, talked about the need for a small hotel/motel to accommodate business people who lived in the area for 6 months (i.e., October through March) while training horses for harness racing. They also believed that a small hotel/motel would accommodate visitors who came to the community for other business or tourism during the other 6 months (April through September). They discussed the idea for 4 or 5 years, had a study conducted by a nearby 2-year college, and then were able to share their conviction with information (study) to a local businessman who built a 28 unit motel. It is our belief that without the continuing discussion, conviction, and commitment to providing hotel/motel accommodations in the community, their studies would have sat on the shelf and never been implemented.

Being Proactive versus Reactive

Communities that listen to the needs of existing business and industries, seek out information about how to improve the downtown, actively cooperate with a cross section of special interest groups, and design strategies for community change are being proactive. They are working in the present and future (see Figure 1.1, The chronological planning trap). Groups that wait for the impact of some regulation or change at the state or federal level are being reactive. Before a large manufacturing plant in Albany, Georgia, closed, community and statewide developers had already begun a search for other businesses that could employ a skilled labor force plus use the soon to be abandoned facilities. In contrast, waiting too long to begin recruiting another industry, can be disastrous. From a different perspective, Wrightsville, Georgia, was also proactive in developing a video tape about the community resources for retirees. When developers came to town looking for a fast food restaurant location, they also saw the video tape and were convinced that the community was forward-thinking and proactive. Since that time the fast food restaurant is in operation, a new health care (two-doctor clinic) facility has been built, the train depot has been renovated, and the group is looking for someone to build a small to medium size hotel/motel for families who might visit relatives at a 1200 bed state corrections institution.

Selling Your Community

Groups that use every opportunity to market their community develop a successful track record. Examples include using a video tape about retirees and sending it to cities in the United States with cable television; showing the same video to investors and developers (Wrightsville, Georgia); promoting your town, museums, music shows, and other attractions on public and commercial radio that reaches I-75 (Buena Vista, Georgia); marketing speciality foods (peanut butter) to other communities in the United States (Lumpkin, Georgia); using local artists to capture unique community features, such as, church steeples on greeting cards, calendars, and prints (Abbeville, South Carolina); selling a book about the Swamp Gravy play (Colquitt, Georgia); selling t-shirts that promote London, Paris, New York, and Bogart; inviting state welcome center directors into your community to learn about and experience the area (Buena Vista, Georgia); and providing t-shirts or caps to residents who travel out-of-county and out-of-state (Mayhaw Festival, Colquitt, Georgia). Proactive community groups are always looking for ways to market their community.

BELIEVE IT!

The saying goes, if you don't believe it can happen it probably won't happen! Without a vision of the future and a belief that people can make things happen in your community, you are wasting your time, it is that simple. Communities with people who have faith, are future oriented, take time to plan, believe that they can be successful, and work toward achieving their goals, are successful.

SUMMARY

What is so different about community economic development described in this chapter? We believe the differences are most often how the community does four things:

1. Develops broad based *support* from residents throughout the community;

2. Creates a *shared vision* of what community change is and your part of that vision;

3. Establishes a *climate for individual and group learning* from each other and about the community; and

4. Promotes a *willingness to work together* across political, social, racial, and economic boundaries.

There are always discussions of what distinguishes successful communities from those that are not as successful in community economic development. The list on page 153 contains factors that characterize successful community economic development. Again, from our experiences, these are the factors that stand out as important in the successful communities in which we have worked and which we have read about. How do your action planning efforts measure up? We encourage you to give these items a try!

PROMOTING SUCCESSFUL COMMUNITY ECONOMIC DEVELOPMENT

- Using a broad based community vision not just individual leadership.
- Not using the lack of money as an excuse for doing nothing.
- Being visible and positive by using a proactive strategy.
- Making local investments and commitments before asking outsiders for their investments and commitments.
- Providing a wide variety of ways for local people to get involved.
- Including a broad cross-section of people (not the usual suspects) for ideas and participation.
- Being persistent in knocking on doors and asking for help.
- Not quickly dismissing an idea, suggestion, or project.
- Trying a wide variety of ways to get the project done.
- Making it a point to know what others know about your community.
- Knowing the importance of dressing for success . . . having your community looking successful and prosperous.
- Committing to work on the "ugly babies" in the community.
- Learning from your own and others' successes and failures.
- Being willing to change and do it differently than in the past.
- Working together as community organizations and groups, sharing and celebrating recognition.
- Specifying success from a community perspective.
- Realizing that success does not follow a cookbook . . . being willing to change the recipe to fit the local community need.
- Not waiting for studies before starting a project.
- Using every opportunity to sell your community.
- Believing development can happen . . . and it will.

CHAPTER 10

Utilizing Resources and Building Networks

Byte, bits, ram, rom, cd, networks, fiber optics, satellite, large dish, small dish, no dish, interactive, distance learning, menus, mosaics, gophers, webs, and so on (Burrus, 1993; Campbell & Ndubisi, 1994; Halal & Liebowitz, 1994; Verity & Hof, 1994; Wagner, 1994). Our technology vocabulary changes from day to day. Keeping up with technological change is almost out of control. Futurists predict that the world's knowledge at the turn of the century will double every 32 days! How can we possibly keep up with changes in technology, learning, and the impacts these changes will have on our everyday lives? If you think about it too long, it becomes frustrating. These frustrations are heightened in communities where residents see the need for change and for updating their technical skills or knowledge but don't know where to start. Who should they contact? Where can they go for help? Whoa! Wait a minute. This is about using resources and building networks to promote economic development and change in communities. Where should we start?

ORDER OUT OF CHAOS

Some authors (Peters, 1988; Peters & Waterman, 1982) would have you believe that chaos is necessary for change and development. Others like Senge (1990, 1994) seem to indicate that if we analyze the situation, there is some order in what is going on around us or at least we can try to impose some order so we can move forward. Probably both points of view are correct. At the very least, they are evident in our everyday lives such as in our work, learning, leisure, and community involvement.

Utilizing resources is something many people in the 1990s, especially those in the United States, believe they are expert at doing by generating monies, support, and human energy for making projects happen. For example, several jurisdictions across the United States have merged city and county public services to make more efficient use of resources. Many states have in place regional agencies for education services such as Board of Cooperative Educational Services (BOCES), Regional Educational Service Agencies (RESAs), and for community planning Regional Development Commissions (RDCs) and other area planning agencies. All of these networks and coalitions are aimed at trying to get efficient use out of scarce resources.

The changing technology available to us has also changed the way communities look at marketing. A wide and ever changing, variety of marketing tools is at your disposal depending upon your creativity. You can seek to present your community to prospective customers indirectly through media advertising. You can attempt to reach them directly by using directed letters, brochures, or videotapes sent to their offices or by using telemarketing techniques. One community with which we have worked, Wrightsville, Georgia, produced a short video that they offered to cable systems as part of their community programming.

You can exhibit in trade shows and conventions attended by executives of business and industry. You can host meetings in your community, or with other communities, and invite potential business or industrial prospects to join you for a combined presentation and social event. You can make marketing trips and visit executives of businesses at their offices.

The tools you use will be determined in part by the nature of what you have to promote, the community's current image among developers or those to whom you are promoting, and in part, by the resources available to you. Each of these techniques

have proponents and detractors. Some professionals are convinced that media advertising has little impact. Others can
document good leads generated by targeted advertising programs. Some economic developers swear by direct mail cam-
paigns, others have given up on them. Very few have tried extensive telemarketing, using satellite and video productions.
There is no right way to make contacts that suit all communities. Determine who you are trying to reach and what kind of
message you need to deliver to get the attention of your targeted
audience. Then choose a set of tools that is best suited to the
delivery of that message to your audience. Given changes in
technology, how you use the "information superhighway" to
your advantage will indicate a lot about your technological
savvy as a community and your success in the future.

PUTTING IT ALL TOGETHER

This chapter describes the rationale for our efforts to help
communities adjust to changing socioeconomic circumstances
and presents some tools that can be used in providing that help.
Taken together, these tools constitute an economic development
action plan that has the potential to broaden a community's job
base and thereby soften the inevitable loss of jobs in traditional
industries whose employment levels are contracting. But no action plan achieves its objectives without committed people willing to carry it out or without the financial and other resources
needed to execute the necessary tasks.

Building a Consensus for Change

Even the best conceived community economic development action plan is of no value if those who must implement
each change and those who will be influenced by the changes
are not committed to the undertaking. There are very few company towns left in this country, and there are few political
bosses capable of dictating a community's agenda. Coalitions

must be built. To build an effective coalition, those who are committed to an economic development effort must gain the cooperation and support of key business leaders, elected and appointed government officials, a wide variety of community groups, and the media through rational and thorough discussions of the risks of not acting and the opportunities to be gained by community action.

Building Networks for Community Economic Development

Chambers of commerce (Kinsella, 1989) are located in cities, towns, and regions across the United States. They exist to improve the business climate and overall social and economic well-being of a community. A chamber of commerce is a network of local business people who want to see the community develop to improve their business opportunities. Obviously, there is a relationship between the well being of businesses in a given community and the well being of the people who live and work in the city, town, or region. Chambers of commerce promote their members and the services they bring to a community or region. Chamber members help to recruit other businesses, especially those they need for suppliers. As the critical mass of business development in the form of services, manufacturing, product design, transportation, entertainment, food, clothing, and housing increases so do needs for education and public services. Community economic development is one way to begin raising the perception that "this is a good community in which to live and work because there are jobs, services, education, recreation, churches, and a host of other quality of life factors that are important."

Most communities have several organizations with a role or at least a vested interest in efforts to strengthen the local economy. In many communities, the chamber of commerce is the primary agent in this undertaking. In others, a unit of local government or a commission funded by local government plays this role. In some areas, a form of public/private coalition has been created with support from the chamber of commerce and the local government to assure coordinated community action from both groups. Occasionally the industrial development authority or private industry council, groups created to coordinate industry solicitation and job training activities, will lead efforts to create jobs. In many states, regional development authorities have sometimes assumed this role for member communities.

Regardless of who takes the lead role in local economic development, all of these organizations usually participate in some way in the effort. Other participants have included local banks, utilities, colleges and universities, and real estate developers. In some communities, efforts are carefully coordinated and orchestrated. In other communities, concern over who gets credit for success produces competition rather than cooperation. In these communities, there is usually little success for which to take credit. There is no right way to organize for a community's economic development program. The character of the community and the nature of the working relationships in it will determine what gets done. It is important that all parties agree to a common agenda and that they control their individual interests and rules to the common good of the community.

THE ON-LINE NETWORK OR INTERNET

A recent *Business Week* article about the Internet (Verity & Hof, 1994) describes how anyone anywhere with a computer, modem (access to telecommunications), and time can gather and exchange information, advertise products and services, search other networks, and build special interest networks with like-minded users in a matter of minutes. Also, these networks are not bounded by a neighborhood, city, or town but they can be interstate, multistate, national, and international in scope. W. I. Thomas's famous statement (roughly stated), "Whatever the mind can perceive it can design," is truer today than at any other time in the history of man. Technology is providing multiple interactive techniques for people to learn, design, develop, promote, and market almost anything imaginable. Community economic developers can use these same resources through the Internet, and its future replacements, to find information and help for transforming their communities. One such example is the numerous community freenets (Maciuszko, 1990), springing up on the Internet almost daily. New Mexico, Indiana, New York, Illinois, and North Carolina seem to be leading the way in the development of these freenets.

Applying the Internet to
Community Economic Development

If the basics of community economic development are people solving their own problems in real time by learning about their situation, exploring options, discussing alternatives, selecting and trying out options, evaluating results, and putting this new knowledge back to work on other problems, then the new age of interactive technology is a natural fit for this type of action learning. Community problem solvers can now meet and discuss issues that are of local concern, such as solid waste disposal, the design of a greenway along a stream in the community, or the location of a new highway that will compliment the existing transportation system with others in nearby or distant locations, without ever leaving home.

Community groups are no longer in the dark about what laws exist that would impact their decisions or what other communities anywhere in the world would have done about solving similar problems. The Internet can be a tool for gathering information, for sharing information, and for locating legal or other guidelines for successful resolution of the same or similar problems. It may be possible to travel via virtual reality and video tapes at one location to other community problem solver locations and inform the group about available options and alternatives. The interactive nature of the Internet and related technologies could give community problem solvers more information and knowledge about their situation before spending their time and money visiting unrelated or unsuccessful sites. There is no shortage of various discussion groups on the Internet (listservers) that one can join. The list of topics is virtually unlimited. One caution however, be prepared for voluminous amounts of Internet junk mail. Even this technology has its drawbacks!

WHERE IS THE TECHNOLOGY GOING?

For the past few years, the technology has focused on two modes: satellites and cable. In some cases access to satellites has required the use of cable. Satellite technology is moving rapidly from the large solid or wire mesh dishes to the small, 18 to 24 inches in diameter, dishes that offer more options than 10 of the older large dish systems combined. Eventually, dishes may be hand held 6 to 8 inch diameter types that can be carried in a fanny pack. It is also possible that satellite technology could be outdistanced by cable as new advances are made in sending information, data, text, etc., along copper wires and fiber optic cable. Officials at the Ellijay Telephone Company recently shared with us information about research at Bell Labs that has expanded the capability of using copper wire to send 200 times the volume as in the past. This is an astounding breakthrough in technology.

Who Has the Technology . . .
Who Can Get the Technology?

The battle between small and large telecommunications systems rages in the news media on a daily basis. The large carriers have more money for advertising than the smaller systems thus we hear more from them. However, small telecommunications systems must be more customer oriented and must look for more efficiency in their service delivery. Discussions with several small telecommunications companies in Georgia and other states indicate that they have up-to-date technology, such as digital switching and fiber-optic cable, that is very competitive with larger carriers. Further, small telecommunications systems are often more willing to reconfigure and redesign their systems to meet the special needs of customers.

We are convinced that many rural communities are not as far out of the technological mainstream as some would have you believe. Our experience indicates that smaller progressive telecommunications organizations have developed a history of customer orientation in order to compete with larger companies.

What Does the Community Do to Build Networks?

First, find out what telecommunications technology exists within and near your community. What are the special telecommunications needs of existing business or industry, and what is available for modern industries that are moving into other locations within your community? Talk to the telecommunications businesses about what exists now, and how to get new technology and plan for future technology.

Several communities we have visited are using two-way audio/video (distance learning), cable, satellite, fiber optic, computer networks, and anything else they can learn about and acquire. They want existing businesses and industries as well as new business moving into the area to have the necessary technology now rather than a promise that the technology will be delivered at a later date.

EXAMPLE: A RURAL COMMUNITY THAT IS NETWORKED

Currently the technology exists to create networked communities that connect residents literally to the global village. When the developers/owners of ACME Business Products and Services (ACME/BPS) were looking for a place to locate their business, they could have picked any community they wanted. Company needs were about 40,000 square feet of manufacturing space, 20,000 square feet service/office space, and 10,000 square feet of administrative office space. All three activities would need to be networked (could use local area networks, LANs) and then it would be desirable to have direct connections to suppliers. Also, ACME/BPS would build a network of their service personnel and their customers as they were added to the operations. Because of annual inspections of ACME Products and the need to keep records of servicing these products, it is necessary to build an interactive network of customers. In the past 5 years ACME/BPS had promoted a system where customers could contact each other to share information about ACME/BPS products and services.

New technology is being developed for ACME/BPS that will require regular contacts with South African and New Zealand designers and German fabricators. Company field personnel have requested that they and selected customers be able to review the design, fabrication, and preliminary testing of the new technology.

All of these interactive discussions between the international technology suppliers/developers with the company and company to staff and customers has created a communications pattern that could not be easily done on typewriters and paper. However, these communications are relatively simple with E-mail, fax, Internet, and other international communications networks.

Also, the local chamber of commerce would like to include ACME/BPS on the community net to keep owners, employees, and customers in contact with other businesses in the area and region. The chamber publishes a newsletter and reports of major events, and they keep in daily contact with businesses regarding labor shortages, health care and accidents, visitors to their work sites that might be interested in expanding or locating a facility in their community, and emergencies that might arise.

It should be pointed out that all of the community public

health providers (e.g., hospitals, clinics, and EMTs), safety services (e.g., fire and police protection), and transportation systems (e.g., air, water, roads, and highways) are also networked and can be notified by anyone in the community.

One of the strengths of ACME/BPS that allows them to compete with other producer/service companies is their access to an information/data/problem solving center located at the local technical school. Because all of the school systems are networked with the community, ACME/BPS can describe an existing problem or an anticipated problem by monitoring selected indicators and share these with the production problems class at the technical school. They have an added knowledge base of 15 students and 2 instructors who can help with problem-solving. Technical school students also participate in the community internship program and learn about different business and industries in the area.

Once a month the chamber sponsors an on-line network round table for 2 hours where individuals in the community, such as, business, industry, and public schools, talk with someone at the state capitol or a consultant or university resource about a variety of communication, production, service, or related issues. In addition, the chamber can periodically poll members about economic issues in the community.

Roundtables are also conducted on other issues as well. For example, International Cultural Olympiad groups conducted some of their preliminary scheduling via interactive audio/visual networks. Neighboring communities have sponsored institutes about a variety of topics, such as native American folklore; genealogy; preserving our heritage by identifying and placing homes, buildings, and other locations on the national register; fund-raising for nonprofit organizations; and improving the hospitality skills of everyone in the community to promote tourism. Just recently it has been noticed that several companies in the community are beginning to coordinate deliveries for shipping products and receiving supplies. This has contributed to considerable savings for several of the small and recent start-up businesses in the area.

SUMMARY

Modern telecommunications will increasingly be the way that you market your community. The "worldwide web" will be a direct link to regional, national, and international contacts. Virtual reality technology, digital cameras, and photographic equipment mounted on personal computers will offer an ever-expanding array of options to promote and market your community. To become a "networked" community, more and more of the residents must become familiar with and begin using the available interactive telecommunications technology. You will need to challenge local public school personnel, business organizations, and community leaders to use and secure the necessary hardware and software to engage in this important dialogue. For example, you can develop your own home page, put together a digitized videotape of your community's assests, and develop the digital backup information to introduce visitors to your area. A local task force of volunteers, community leaders, and technology experts can keep the community up to date on the daily improvements and changes in telecommunications.

TIPS FOR UTILIZING RESOURCES
AND BUILDING NETWORKS

For communities that want to take advantage of telecommunications technology to improve or establish their competitive advantage the answer is to get started YESTERDAY! Do not wait for the costs to go down or the stock market to reach a certain level or any other signal. Do it now without delay! Consider doing the following:

1. Inventory your existing community telecommunications capabilities such as fiber optics, cable, satellite dishes at public facilities, and business/industry.
2. Determine how your community or creative individuals are currently accessing other networks and on-line services for pay and free services.
3. Determine how your community or creative individuals are networked to communicate with themselves, their constituencies, education, government, business, industry, public safety, other communities, and what you have in the way of distance learning sites or access to such sites.
4. Check with current employers and other organizations in the community about their current and future communications needs.
5. Inventory the utilities such as gas, electric, water, phone, and cable that currently deliver services to your community.
6. Identify an individual or group, class, or special interests that keeps up with the latest innovations in communications technology that would be beneficial to a community wanting to expand its economic development capability.
7. Share information within the community both by face-to-face meetings and via E-mail or telecommunications. Keep as many in the community informed as possible.

8. Consider offering information and referral services such as networking within the community to chamber of commerce members, merchants' association members, public schools and colleges, community boards, elected officials, and others in the community.

CHAPTER 11

Future Strategies for Enhancing Community Economic Development

Hopefully, we have convinced you that community economic development should be an important topic among a large cross section of your community's citizenry. However, many times we find that local folks are unclear and confused about how socioeconomic changes and trends in the international, national, and state economies are affecting their local community job opportunities, what kinds of jobs are available, and where they can be found. In many communities, money issues such as rising prices, declining incomes, or job loss, command the attention of the average citizen. When these issues also negatively affect the quality of life of a community, the vibrancy and vitality of a community, the local tax base of a community, or local tax revenues, community citizens and local political leaders begin to take notice.

What confuses and concerns community groups with whom we work are the numerous interpretations of what these important socioeconomic trends are and the various assessments of their relative magnitude of impact on a local community's economy and its ability to create jobs. Among the important, confusing, and troublesome socioeconomic trends we see community groups identify are (Brooks, 1991, May):

1. Concern with foreign competition and trade practices, including confusion over NAFTA and GATT

2. Worries about increasing automation, technological change, restructuring, and layoffs in the workplace

3. Perception of eroding of support for and investment in vocational education

4. Notions of the declining quality of primary and secondary education in their community and the United States

5. Alarm over the lack of a concerted policy emphasis on the nation's industrial development given changes in domestic and international industrial competitiveness during the 1980s and 1990s

6. Dismay with tax codes that seem to discourage capital investment in retooling manufacturing in the United States

7. Constantly changing personal preferences about where and how people want to live and work

In reality, all of these factors contribute to a dramatic and often traumatic economic transformation of local community economies. The bottom line is that the social and economic rules guiding community economic development are changing for almost everyone in the world, as well as for most Americans. However, we believe strongly that how responsive and innovative your community is to these changes will affect your community's ability to provide good jobs for local citizens and go a long way toward determining the economic and social stability of your community.

SOME CURRENT ISSUES

Looking into the future is an uncertain business. If we begin with some issues and trends we may be able to find some degree of precision. In this chapter we are compiling a list of issues, ideas, and trends that we have seen over the past 25 years. Added to this information are notions and suggestions gleaned from research and popular literature about community needs and economic trends or forecasts. Also, we have included some insights which we have gathered from working with community groups during the past few years that have generated both concern and high-spirited discussions about what we need to prepare for in the future.

Views

First, there is a dichotomy of views about what people can do to improve their community economic conditions. One view is that community members should decide what they want to do regarding community improvements and changes. Other views suggest that expert community developers and economic strategists should tell the community what it needs to work on to improve its economic position, because they have special skills or special knowledge and know what the community needs. Our view entails a bottoms-up process which implies that locals know what needs to change.

Knowledge

Second, there is a related issue that community change is driven by numbers, data, facts, and statistics that clearly specify a need or direction. In Chapter 2 (Figure 2.1) we have described what we believe is the role of information, data, and facts and how this becomes knowledge that can be used in decision making. We believe that residents have knowledge about their communities that can be supported by information and data. We also believe that residents can benefit from outside points of view or consultants or technical assistance if they invest their time in forming the questions for experts to answer. Challenge the expert or outside resource to think about local problems and offer several options for decision making that reflect the energy and scope of the local community.

Collective Vision

A third issue or concern is getting people in a community or members from a variety of communities to bridge the "me" or "mine" or special interest turf to thinking about what we can do as a collective of skilled, interested and capable people who can bring about change in a given area. When people realize they have skills, knowledge, and expertise and that they can work together to achieve a collective vision or goal, they become a powerful energy force that can get the job done.

Time

A fourth issue is convincing individuals and groups that they need to take the time to work on an issue or topic or dilemma. One of the first hurdles we have to overcome with any group is time. Most directors, presidents, or chief officers of community groups start out their conversations with us about time. For example, "We want you to help our committee (or group) understand the nuts and bolts of community economic development but please do this in 20 minutes during our luncheon and before we adjourn to play golf." If a community or group or organization does not want to take the time to work on the problem then there is no problem or no vision or both!

Change

A fifth issue, is that communities, organizations, or groups that have invested time to discuss, wrestle with, and hammer out a vision of the future WILL get things done. They will make some changes in their community. The reason they will achieve their goals or vision is that everybody involved has a vested interest in the change, and they all know what their role is in making change happen. Without a clear view of who does what for whom and when, there is no organized energy force for change.

Follow-up

A sixth issue focuses on the overall action learning/planning process. This is where groups learn to follow up on their goals and vision and create strategies for managing time and resources used in achieving their vision. When groups build in check points of information exchange, review, and reorganizing to move ahead, they learn individually and collectively. These many little steps and activities add up to something bigger. They also learn that other strategies may be needed to ensure accomplishment.

Resources

Lastly, we suggest that groups consider funding, monies, technical assistance, and gathering resources. We don't list this as a first concern or issue because when it is identified by the group as the major hurdle or barrier, the group creates a seemingly insurmountable barrier to developing a vision or goal with any degree of enthusiasm. After the group understands the desired change, the rationale for the change, and the impact the change will have on people and the environment, they can wrestle with the funding and resources. Oftentimes the group has a better view of what resources are needed and how they can secure the support for changes they have a passion and conviction about. When community groups get excited about what needs to change to make their community a better place to live and to support business development, they look beyond the dollar signs and begin to think about what should be and what must be and what will benefit the entire community.

COMMUNITY ECONOMIC
DEVELOPMENT TRENDS

Local community members and decision makers are being challenged with more difficult problems. Regulations, standards, best practices, management approaches, and concern for human beings are the factors facing local decision makers. Community members need to have skills, training, and experience in problem solving and decision making at all levels or to draw upon experiences in other facets of the community, e.g., boards, committees, groups, or organizations outside of work, to assist in problem solving (Chapter 3). Most of these challenges arrive at the office, home, or community without adequate funding or support (Chapter 8). The problems need to be solved, but they are often unfunded or underfunded, and the burden lies with the local community.

Joint Ventures

Community groups may want to check-in with nearby communities or counties to see if a joint or regional venture for development is feasible. Baker City, Oregon (described in Chapter 6), and Crawfordville, Georgia (described in Chapter 6) are examples of communities reaching out to nearby communities to develop joint ventures. Community, organizational, and multijurisdictional cooperatives offer opportunities and possible funding mechanisms that may not be possible for a single organization or unit.

Both local leaders and volunteers must get information and training to solve their own technical assistance problems. Community groups may need to bring in statewide developers, expertise from banking, utilities, state agencies, and possibly universities. One approach that has worked well for us is getting the community group to sit down and discuss their technical assistance needs with university public service faculty. These discussions have resulted in locating faculty and students who are supervised in designing specific projects and processes that enable the community to move forward and also give students a real live project to include in their experience portfolio. University faculty are looking for projects that they can engage their students in to learn and develop new skills.

Telecommunications

New strategies for community economic developers and communities can be addressed using distance learning and telecommunications technologies (Chapter 10). Also, competition is greater because more individuals, agencies, and communities have expertise in using these technologies. For example, recruiting industrial prospects to communities takes on a dimension of telecommunication access in addition to physically locating a facility in a community.

Communities that already have their telecommunications infrastructure in place are better able to compete for attracting businesses or industries that need these technologies. Also, existing businesses and industries can benefit from these networks. We think it would be intriguing for one or more communities to market themselves as a networked environment that is dedicated to starting new businesses. Part of the marketing strategy would be that existing businesses, industries, government, and community support groups are part of this networked environment which may use distance learning, telecommunications, Internet, and other forms of communication.

Role of Manufacturing in Job Development

We recently conducted an economic development educational program for five rural communities. In four of these communities, manufacturing income accounted for 30 percent or more of total labor and proprietor income. For these four communities, major socioeconomic changes are particularly troublesome. You cannot pick up a popular publication devoted to business issues that does not indicate continued declines in manufacturing's share of total employment. Magazines, such as *Business Week* and *Fortune*, predict that the steepest long-term declines are expected in the durable goods sector, for items such as primary metals, furniture, and machinery. Durable goods manufacturing has been the mainstay of many production-based local economies. Many manufacturing industries have lost jobs over the past decade and a half. For example, during the late 1980s the *U.S. Industrial Outlook* pointed out that industries particularly hard hit were durable manufacturing ones in the transportation equipment industries, such as automobiles and aircraft.

The most prevalent economic development concern in many states has been over those communities that have manufacturing plants that produce nondurable goods, such as apparel and textile products. As the U.S. *Industrial Outlook* has pointed out time and again, these plants have experienced large job losses over the past 14 years as labor costs and increased foreign competition have taken their toll. In our state alone, Georgia lost 10,500 jobs during the 1980s in the nondurable manufacturing sector. A closer examination of shifts in employment growth, nationally and across states, underscores the fundamental restructuring that is underway.

What is interesting, is that during the tumultuous times of the late 1970s and 1980s there were manufacturers scattered across the country that maintained a positive rate of growth in the face of growing foreign competition by investing in new technologies that enabled them to increase their productivity at an average of more than 3 percent annually. That translates into jobs. We have been particularly impressed by some of the investment in technology we have seen by some firms producing textile products and apparel. Again, perusal of industry outlooks showed that in the latter part of the 1980s, and continuing into the 1990s, both industries have had success stories where negative job growth rates have been turned around. Many manufacturing plants in Georgia and throughout the United States also remained competitive by shifting a portion of their purchases of intermediate products, which are used in goods assembled here, to offshore suppliers. The auto industry is a good example of this strategy.

Recently, the strategies for community economic development relative to job creation require that we distinguish between industries producing *goods*, such as mining, construction, manufacturing, and agriculture enterprises, and industries producing *services*, such as transportation and public utility firms, wholesale and retail businesses, service firms, government entities, and finance, insurance, and real estate concerns. A very surprising statistic, showing employment in goods producing industries to be fairly constant nationally from 1920 through 1993 (see figure 11.1), emerges. In the post World War II period, employment in the service producing industries began to take off. The result is a service sector more than three times as large as the goods sector of the United States economy in total employment in 1993.

Given the factors of productivity improvement requirements and increasing foreign competition, many communities across the country will find it increasingly difficult to promote expansion of existing and the attraction of new, production facilities each year to offset an average annual decline of 3 to 5 percent in the level of employment needed to support present output. Land availability will be a constraint for some. The shrinking supply of investments in new manufacturing plants will be a constraint for most. Contrary to some current economic development strategies, the pursuit of traditional manufacturing facilities should not completely disappear from your job creation agenda (see Chapter 7). However, be aware of what might happen to manufacturing in the future given the community economic development trends discussed earlier and the answers you should be uncovering to these questions about existing firms in your community and firms you may be recruiting (Brooks, 1991, May):

1. Is the firm in an intermediate phase; outdated in product, plant, or equipment; or planning to relocate where labor is cheaper?

2. Is there, or has there been, a retooling phase in which the company could go from being labor intensive to being capital intensive (automated)?

3. Is the firm highly import sensitive?

4. Is the firm's product highly substitutable?

5. Is the firm's market transitional?

6. Is the firm susceptible to negative regulatory legislation?

7. What sort of community neighbor will the firm be?

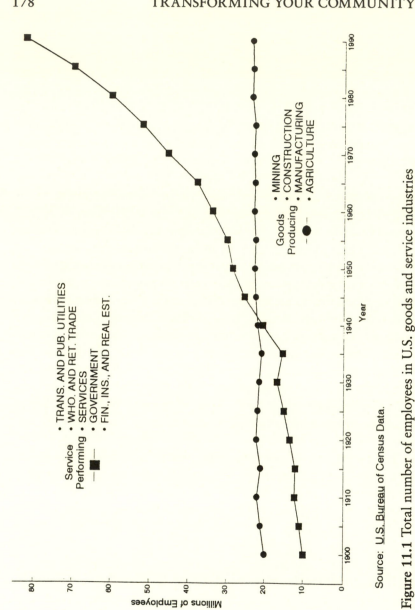

Source: U.S. Bureau of Census Data.

Figure 11.1 Total number of employees in U.S. goods and service industries

Considering that traditional manufacturing industries probably represent a declining employment source, keep in mind that some communities did quite well in attracting and creating manufacturing jobs in the 1980s and early 1990s. Manufacturing jobs will continue to be a vital factor in the overall, economic well-being of most communities, particularly rural communities.

Role of the Service Sector in Job Development

The service sector has increasingly emerged as the critical force driving the economy of many communities across the United States, and we increasingly run into community economic development groups that are concerned with this trend. Service industries, including communications, transportation, wholesale and retail trade, financial services, health care, government, education, and various professional services, employ three out of four Americans on average (*U.S. Bureau of the Census*, 1994). Service sector jobs and output have grown steadily since the early 1950s, even in recessionary periods. Within manufacturing itself, 70 to 75 percent of all jobs are in service activities such as design, accounting, maintenance, and personnel. Some of the most successful ventures of the 1980s, including Home Depot, Southern Bell, and Chick-Fil-A, are service firms. And many of the most successful new manufacturers, such as Hayes, Wellington Leisure Products, and Scientific Atlanta, sell primarily to service industries.

A strong service sector is a natural and desirable complement to your community's manufacturing sector and an outgrowth of the sophisticated application of technology to service activities. Major companies such as NationsBank, Southern Bell, and Turner Communications have demonstrated that service companies can use technology as effectively as manufacturing companies to improve productivity, increase profits, and gain competitive advantage. Indeed, large service companies are comparable to large manufacturing enterprises in the amount of capital they invest in each worker and in the value each worker adds to the Gross National Product (GNP). The ability of the service sector to continue increasing its productivity through the use of technology will be a critical factor in the future performance of your community's and the United States economy.

Interaction of Manufacturing and the Service Sector

Much of the conventional wisdom about the service sector does not pertain to your local economy. The growth of the service sector is neither a cause nor a by-product of a decline in manufacturing jobs across the country. Rather, services have created new markets for manufactured goods and substantially helped improve manufacturing efficiency, as seen in the increase of manufacturing jobs in states like South Carolina and Georgia during the 1980s and early 1990s. Particularly misleading is the view that service firms depend almost entirely upon manufacturing firms for markets. The two sectors are mutually interdependent, so much so that it is counterproductive to think about community economic development strategies for one without considering the other. Many service companies exist largely in support of manufactured goods providing for their transportation, financing, advertising, repair, or distribution. But there is the less recognized fact that service firms provide the major markets for many manufactured goods. For example, a large part of all manufactured high technology machinery, communications equipment, and health care products are sold to the service sector.

Manufacturers in most communities are also heavily dependent on other services, such as market research, computer-aided design and "just-in-time" distribution systems, to adapt and present their products effectively in the changing marketplace. Because global competition has expanded in recent years, success in manufacturing depends increasingly on the ability to respond quickly and creatively to market feedback. By linking themselves more directly to their markets through service technologies, many of your community's manufacturers can offer their products throughout the United States with advantages that overseas producers cannot.

We often hear that textile and apparel producers cannot compete with the fabrics produced in low wage countries, but parts of the textile and apparel industry are beginning to turn this pattern around. We have had the opportunity to visit with some textile and apparel manufacturers who are moving full steam ahead. The last several years have begun to show some increase in the number of jobs in these industries. Affluence has led to rapidly changing, greatly differentiated, fashions in response to highly individualized tastes, creating major new opportunities for alert producers.

Some companies have begun to integrate their operations electronically to coordinate fiber production, fabric manufacture, and distribution thereby substantially reducing inventory costs as well as eliminating expensive delays in reaching the market. Computer-aided design and manufacturing links between cutters in one part of the country and mills in another part of the country can halve the time between the design of a new garment and the delivery of finished products.

In an increasingly competitive environment, effective application of service technologies can give your community's firms the advantages in efficiency and responsiveness that more than offset foreign producers' advantages in labor costs. An excellent example of how all this is happening is provided by the reemergence of cotton production in the United States and the development of permanent press cotton garments. Stop in any clothing store and notice the growth in these items. We predict tremendous growth in this sector over the next few years.

Conclusions

You need to be aware that there are important conclusions to be reached regarding trends in service sector and manufacturing sector jobs in your community. Many people have misread employment trends and predicted dire consequences for the future economic well-being of many communities. The job numbers are not increasing for manufacturing jobs at the rate they are for services, but we see that manufacturing is undergoing many structural changes, which over the next decade, may place that sector in a cost competitive position within a world market where many sellers have lower labor costs. Unfortunately, it will result in the loss of a number of jobs.

There are still indications from a number of sources that the manufacturing sector in some communities has yet to emerge from the recessionary mode of the early 1990s. Again, we think your emphasis should focus on being informed about trends and conditions in the larger economy so you can better assist the local and area manufacturing sector in its efforts to restructure in terms of those factors that will make it competitive. Statistics from the *U.S. Industrial Outlook,* the U.S. Department of Labor's *Monthly Labor Review,* or from publications such as *Business Week* and *Fortune* do not indicate the demise of manufacturing as an important contributor to unemployment. Neither do these statistics chronicle the emergence of a hamburger stand economy, with retail outlets selling to each other and consumers and offering low wage, low skill jobs, in which the standard of living will inevitably erode as incomes decline. The challenge is to encourage more accurate descriptions of job growth around your state and community.

Many service jobs offer wages and salaries comparable to those in manufacturing. The service sector includes people working in business and professional services; repair services; finance, insurance, and real estate services; and health services. They provide exportable services that can bring new money into local economies, so they can substitute for jobs lost in the manufacturing segment of any local economy.

Business and professional service firms tend to locate in communities offering viable local markets that serve as a foundation from which they can also pursue export markets. Traditionally, manufacturing establishments have been a principal market for these service firms. Academic institutions and large state and federal government operations are other markets for business and professional services.

Consequently, unless a community is close to a large urban area or to academic or governmental institutions, it will have trouble retaining or enlarging its business service employment base in the face of a potentially eroding manufacturing sector. Even though manufacturers may not be a prime source of new jobs, their role as business service consumers will continue to be critical to the economic vitality of most communities. Manufacturing's contribution to your local economy must be measured more in terms of output and consumption than on the basis of employment in the future.

COMMUNITY ECONOMIC DEVELOPMENT FUTURES

Given what we have talked about throughout this book, we see the following as determinants of successful community economic development:

1. A sharing of expertise and workers across community, county, city, and state lines

2. Education, experience, and training in problem solving and decision making

3. Formation of coalitions, collaborative endeavors, and cooperatives for community economic development

4. Acquisition of technical assistance from a variety of agencies and consultants

5. Enhanced telecommunications networking for learning about community economic development activities

Community economic development is more than just business, industry, and job creation, it is about discovering and developing the entire range of features that causes a *place* to be designated as a *community*.

Community economic development is both a process and a product that calls for an approach that is cognizant of such traditional strategies as industrial recruitment, but attentive to other opportunities such as we have described in this book. Communities that have a vision of where they want to go and put an action learning/planning model in place can be successful in the business of creating businesses, jobs, and an improved quality of life for all its citizens.

REFERENCES

Becker, G. (1975). *Human capital* (3rd. ed.) University of Chicago Press.

Bloomberg, W., Jr., (1966). Community organization. In H. S. Becker (Ed.), *Social problems: A modern approach* (pp. 359–424). New York: John Wiley & Sons, Inc.

Brooks, R. (1991, March). Economic Development Strategies for Georgia Communites (Bulletin 1052) Athens: The University of Georgia College of Agriculture.

Brooks, R. (1991, May). Georgia's Economic Development in the 1990's: Targeting Programs (Bulletin 1054) Athens: The University of Georgia College of Agriculture.

Burrus, D. (1993). *Techno-trends: 24 Technologies that will revolutionize our lives.* New York: Harper Collins.

Campbell, D., & Ndubisi, F. (1994). Brainstorming by byte: Planning practice. *Planning,* 60(1), 19–23. Chicago: American Planning Association.

Carnall, C. A. (1990). *Managing change in organizations.* New York: Prentice Hall.

Carver, J. (1990). *Boards that make a difference.* San Francisco: Jossey-Bass.

Cary, L. (Ed.). (1970). *Community development as a process.* Columbia: University of Missouri Press.

Christenson, J. A., & Robinson, J. (1980). *Community development in America.* Ames: Iowa State University Press.

Cline, C. (1984-personal communication). Involving volunteers in community activities.

Cole, B. D. (1994). Baker City, Oregon develops tourism as a springboard for economic development. *Small Town,* 24(6), 4–9.

Collins, J. C., & Porras, J. I. (1994). *Built to last.* New York: Harper Collins.

Conner, D. R. (1993). *Managing at the speed of change*. New York: Vallard Books.

Crow, S. (1995, personal communication). Using disposable cameras as a technique for involving community volunteers.

Economic Development Digest. (November, 1994). *Ten Tips on Writing Foundation Proposals*. National Association of Development Organizations Research Foundation.

Freire, P. (1968). *Pedagogy of the oppressed*. New York: Continuum Publishing.

Gaventa, J. (1980). *Power and powerlessness: Quiescence and rebellion in an Appalachia Valley*. Chicago: University of Illinois Press.

Glance, N. S., & Huberman, B. A. (1994). The dynamics of social dilemmas. *Scientific American, 270*(3), 76–80.

Halal, W. E., & Liebowitz, J. (1994). Telelearning: The multimedia revolution in education. *The Futurist, 28*(6), 21–26.

Holladay, J. M. (1992). *Economic and community development: A southern exposure*. Dayton, OH: Kettering Foundation.

Institute of Community and Area Development (1994). *Conyers, Rockdale County: Interstate 20 corridor study*. Athens University of Georgia.

Jones, D. C. (Ed.). (1994). *Swamp gravy: Folk tales of south Georgia*. Colquitt, GA: Sobek Press.

Kinsella, T. K. (1989). Small area chambers of commerce. *Commentary, 13*(3), 12–19.

Lam, P. K. (1993). *Credos of Yen: Writings of James Yen*. Unpublished dissertation, University of Texas, Austin.

Maciuszko, K. L. (1990). A quiet revolution: Community online systems. *Online, 14*(6), 24–32.

Maurer, R. C., & Christenson, J. A. (1982). Growth and nongrowth orientations of urban, suburban, and rural mayors: Reflections on the city as a growth machine. *Social Science Quarterly, 63*(2), 350–358.

McNamara, K., & Kriesel, W. (1990). Factors that attract retirees to Georgia counties. Faculty Series, 1990–91, Athens: University of Georgia.

Mezirow, J. (1978). *Education for perspective transformation: Women's re-entry programs in community colleges*. New York: Columbia University, Center for Adult Education, Teacher's College.

Moore, A. B., & Feldt, J. A. (1993). *Facilitating community and decision-making groups*. Malabar, Fl: Krieger.

Nadler, L. (1984). *Handbook of human resource development.* New York: Wiley.

Nix, H. L. (1977). *The community and its involvement in the study planning action process* (Rev. ed.) Athens: University of Georgia, Institute of Community and Area Development.

Pedler, M. (1991). *Action learning in progress* (2nd. ed.) England: Grover House.

Peters, T. J., & Waterman, R. H. (1982). *In search of excellence: Lessons from America's best run companies.* New York: Harper and Row.

Peters, T. J. (1988). *Thriving on chaos: Handbook for management revolution.* New York: Alfred A. Knopfer.

Revans, R. (1980). *Action learning: New techniques for management.* London: Blond and Boggs.

Ross, M. G., & Lappin, B. W. (1967). *Community organization: Theory, principles and practice* (2nd. ed.). New York: Harper and Row.

Rural Information Center U.S. Department of Agriculture. (December, 1994). *Steps in the Funding Process.* Center Publication Series No. 38 compiled by Melanie Gardner.

Sanders, I. T. (1966). *The community: An introduction to a social system.* New York: The Ronald Press Company.

Schultz, T. (1961). Investing in human capital. *The American Economic Review, 51*(1), 1–17.

Senge, P. M., Kleiner, A., Roberts, C., Ross, R., & Smith, B. (1994). *The fifth discipline fieldbook: Tools and strategies for building a learning organization.* New York: Doubleday/Currency.

Senge, P. M. (1990). *The fifth discipline: The art and practice of the learning organization.* New York: Doubleday/Currency.

Sills, D. L. (1975). The environmental movement and its critics. *Human Ecology, 3*(1), 1–14.

Stewart, J. (1991). *Managing change through training and development.* London: Kogan Page Limited.

Taylor, I., & Jinks, J. (1992, personal communication). Community vision for Colquitt, Miller County, Georgia.

U.S. Bureau of the Census. *Statistical Abstract of U.S.: 1994* (114th ed.). Washington, DC: U.S. Government Printing Office.

Verity, J. W., & Hof, R. D. (1994, November 14). The internet: How it will change the way you do business. *Business Week.* 80–86, 88.

Wade, J. (1988, personal communication). Survey of Missouri residents.

Waggoner, M. D. (1992). *Empowering networks: Computer conferencing in education.* Englewood Cliffs, NJ: Educational Technology.

Wagner, C. G. (1994). Toward the new millennium: Living, learning and working. *The Futurist, 28*(6), 37–41.

Warren, R. J. (1978). *The community in America.* Chicago: Rand McNally.

Waters, J. (1982). *Sense of place.* Athens, GA: The Institute of Community and Area Development.

Whorton, J. W. (1993). Developing effective community groups. In R. Golembiewski (Ed.), *Handbook of organizational consultation* (pp. 775–782). New York: Mercel Dekker.

Wilkinson, K. P. (1991). The community in rural America. *Rural Sociological Society.* New York: Greenwood Press.

Willits, F. K., Crider, D. M., & Janota, J. O. (1993). *Citizen's viewpoint: Priorities for the 1990s.* University Park, PA: Penn State University, Department of Agricultural Economics and Rural Sociology.

INDEX